# A SHORT ACCOUNT

OF THE

# KUKI-LUSHAI TRIBES

ON THE

# NORTH-EAST FRONTIER

# A SHORT ACCOUNT
OF THE
# KUKI-LUSHAI TRIBES
ON THE
# NORTH-EAST FRONTIER
(Districts Cachar, Sylhet, Nága Hills, Etc., And The North Cachar Hills),
WITH
# AN OUTLINE GRAMMAR
OF THE
## RANGKHOL-LUSHAI LANGUAGE
AND
*A Comparison of Lushai with Other Dialects.*

BY

**C. A. SOPPITT**

GYAN

*Published by*

Gyan Publishing House
5, Ansari Road
Daryaganj, New Delhi-110002
Phone: 011-47034999, 9811692060
E-mail: books@gyanbooks.com

*Distribution Network*
gyanbooks.com
India, USA, Canada, UK, Australia



ISBN: 978-93-6208-337-1 (HB)
First Published, 1887

2nd Impression 2024

*Printed at:* Gyan Press, Delhi.



**A SHORT ACCOUNT OF THE KUKI-LUSHAI TRIBES ON THE NORTH-EAST FRONTIER**

Author: C. A. SOPPITT

# A SHORT ACCOUNT

OF THE

# KUKI-LUSHAI TRIBES

ON THE

## NORTH-EAST FRONTIER

(DISTRICTS CACHAR, SYLHET, NÁGA HILLS, ETC., AND THE NORTH CACHAR HILLS),

WITH

# AN OUTLINE GRAMMAR

OF THE

## RANGKHOL-LUSHAI LANGUAGE

AND

## A Comparison of Lushai with other Dialects.

BY

C. A. SOPPITT,

ASSISTANT-COMMISSIONER, BURMA, LATE SUB-DIVISIONAL OFFICER, NORTH CACHAR HILLS, ASSAM.

SHILLONG:
PRINTED AT THE ASSAM SECRETARIAT PRESS.

1887.

# A SHORT ACCOUNT

OF THE

# KUKI-LUSHAI TRIBES

ON THE

## NORTH-EAST FRONTIER

(IN THE DISTRICTS OF CACHAR, SYLHET, THE NÁGA HILLS, ETC., AND THE NORTH CACHAR HILLS).

BY

C. A. SOPPITT,

ASSISTANT-COMMISSIONER, BURMA, LATE SUB-DIVISIONAL OFFICER, NORTH CACHAR HILLS, ASSAM.

# PREFACE TO ACCOUNT OF THE TRIBES.

In this short history of the people, commonly grouped under the head of "Kuki," the writer has classified the different sects under two main heads. though four tribes are named:—

(*a*) Râṅgkhôl, co-tribe Bêtê, sub-tribes Sakajaib, Langrong, &c.

(*b*) Jansen, co-tribe Tâdôi, sub-tribes Kôtâng, Slûk, &c.

The writer's authority for this grouping is briefly this:—The Râṅgkhôls and their co-tribe and sub-tribes have so much in common, both in language, manners, customs, and system of internal government, as to render it absolutely necessary to take them together. The Jansen's co-tribe and sub-tribes in the same manner are shown to be closely connected.

It then only remains to show cause for the separation of the two main tribes, and why they should not be grouped under one common name. The following conclusive reasons have been given in the "Account of the tribes." First, the Jansens are ruled over by hereditary Rájas, with well-defined rights, whose powers are despotic, and who cannot even intermarry with commoners, while the Râṅgkhôls have a self-government, the post of "headman," "galim," not being hereditary, and the said "headman" being merely the spokesman of the community. Secondly, distinction in language. Thirdly, distinct social laws and customs.

The official terms "old" and "new" Kuki should not be used. The term "Kuki" itself is too well established to be given up, but the writer considers that a far more appropriate title might be assigned the two tribes by designating the one "Râṅgkhôl (Kuki) Lushai," and the other "Jansen (Kuki) Lushai." The old term "Kuki" would be thus retained, and at the same time a large race of people properly classified for ethnological purposes.

Researches undertaken on the Burmese side of the great watershed would greatly facilitate the classifying and grouping of tribes of whose history (except within comparatively recent years) we are entirely ignorant.

An almost boundless field for ethnological research exists on both the Burma and Assam frontiers, and it is to be hoped that each Government officer or private individual, whose opportunities are such as to enable him to ascertain anything of the history, manners, or customs of any particular tribe, will endeavour to note at once the principal linguistic characteristics. By this means, in the course of a few years, tribes now more or less distinct will be traced back to the parent stock and satisfactorily classified.

The various Kuki laws treating on marriage, rights of succession, &c., will, the writer trusts, prove of value to officials in frontier districts, who are often called upon to decide cases in which the tribal customary procedure can be the only guide to a correct decision. In this short account, the writer has only attempted to note the *principal* manners and customs of the tribes. In the course of time, from contact with outsiders, old manners and customs, and even the language, will slowly but surely change, and means by which connecting links between tribes can be established will be lost for ever. It is while the customs handed down from father to son are still intact that a history, however brief, is of value.

Subsequent to the writing of the above, the compiler joined the Burma Commission, and is at present posted on the frontier north of Bhamo (the Mogaong sub-division). Here he has been thrown in contact with Kachyens, Shans, and other tribes bordering the Irrawaddy Valley, but has not seen enough of them to speak with any great certainty on their manners and customs. A few remarks on the people themselves and their movements may, however, be of interest in connection with this work. On the North-East Frontier of India (Assam) it is difficult to trace any of the tribes back to remote date, the people having been much broken up, and, in addition, the country through which the exodus which brought them to the borders took place almost unknown.

The most that can be done is to note manners, customs, modes of internal village government, &c., and to draw up vocabularies and outline grammars while the dialects are still comparatively pure, trusting that further investigation and research on the Burmese borders will produce links enabling the tribes to be traced back to the parent stock. While writing on the Lushais and Kukis, it has been pointed out that some tribes are gradually forcing others from beyond our north-east frontier (India) into Assam, and it is of great interest to note that in Burma the very same thing is taking place on our Yunan-Chinese Frontier.

Within the last year, for example, large numbers of Shans have retreated from Yunan-China territory and settled about Bhamo.

These people speak a different dialect and are more or less distinct from the Shans in the Shan States east of Mandalay. They are temporarily settled about Bhamo, where, under our rule, they are not harassed, and are in many ways useful to Government. They are a fine, manly-looking race. It is possible that these people will settle permanently in the plains; but had the exodus from Chinese territory taken place during the Burmese rule, it is highly probable that, in preference to placing themselves under that rule, they would have crossed the Irrawaddy, and settled in the hills to the west, the watershed of Burma and Assam.

To make room for them, some of the Kachyen and other tribes (Kukis, Lushais) would have had to move forward westward (that they could successfully have opposed the occupation is not at all likely) pressing forward in their turn others, until the north-east frontier was reached. In other words, on the Burma side of the watershed is to this day seen the commencement of movements which take effect on the Assam frontier years later.

The Burma frontier north of Bhamo, bordering China eastwards and the Patkoi range and Singpho country north, is a most interesting field for ethnological research. The Kachyens bordering the plains to the west of the Irrawaddy bear a great resemblance in many ways to the Nágás, Lushais (Kukis), &c. Their worship is much the same and general mode of life quite in keeping with what is seen on the Assam frontier.

They are not Buddhists like most of the Shans and some Singphos and Kamptis.

This term "Singpho," or "Singphaw," it is stated, is used by some of the Kachyens as their tribal designation, and it is therefore likely that the people commonly spoken of by that name should be mentioned by some other term.

Another tribe living in the plains north of Bhamo may be said to have been more or less recently formed. These people, called "Shans," and so calling themselves, though they occasionally use the term "Phoong," have a different language from the Shans proper and the Burmese, though in manners, dress, and belief they are nearly allied to the latter. They might be described as Shan-Burmese. They occupy a number of the villages about the great plains, thirty miles north of Bhamo, near Magaong and the Endawgjee, or Big Lake.

All these tribes, in common with the Burmese themselves, are of Mongolian origin. The latter, when leaving the northern valleys and settling in the plains of Burma, had much the same species of worship as now prevails among Kachyens, Nágas, Lushais, &c. The date of the introduction of the Buddhist faith into China and Burma may aid considerably in fixing approximately the age *before* which the numerous Mongolian tribes now occupying the vast watershed of the Brahmaputra and the Irrawaddy, first crossed over from China.

From Burmese annals (Boodha Gautha) it would appear that the faith was introduced about the end of the fourth century of our era.

From Chinese annals it would seem that the doctrines were propagated in some parts of that empire in the middle of the first century of our era. At any rate, during the 11th and 12th centuries the religion as regards Burma had reached a great degree of splendour. It is, therefore, fair to presume that eight or ten centuries ago the doctrines of the faith were firmly rooted throughout Burma and China. Subsequent to the establishment of this faith in the two countries it is doubtful whether any tribe, living between the two, would remain long without embracing the new doctrine, in the same manner that the hill people, brought frequently and constantly into contact with the plains of India, invariably embrace some form of Hinduism. We have examples of this in the Shans and others lying between Burma and China, nearly all, if not all, being Buddhists. To the westward, however, between Burma and Assam, the tribes, with the exception of some Singphos (to the north-west) and the Kamtis, are not Buddhist.

From this it may, perhaps, be inferred that the tribes occupying the watershed crossed from China or east of the Irrawaddy previous to the introduction of the Buddhist doctrines, that is to say, more than eight or ten centuries ago. It will probably be argued that the mere fact of crossing from east to west did not exempt a tribe from the influence of the faith, but this can be explained by the nature of the country. East of the Irrawaddy caravan routes have been established with China, &c., from time immemorial, and consequently influence through traders would constantly be brought to bear on tribes, submontane and others.

On the other hand, once settled in the hills to the west of the Irrawaddy, caravans would not visit them, and their intercourse with the plains would be limited to an occasional cold season trip. The Kachyens, for example, do not have much intercourse with the plains, though bordering Burma, and they are not Buddhists, yet some Singphos and the Kamptis living further north, and at present quite out of the influence of the Burmese, profess the faith. This would point to the fact that the Singphos crossed over at a more recent date and subsequent to the introduction of the Buddhist faith, there being no one tribe immediately about them now from whom they could have acquired the doctrines. Briefly, it appears probable that any tribe lying between Burma and China subsequent to the spread of the Buddhist faith would very soon adopt it, and that the fact of certain tribes not having adopted it would point to the exodus having taken place prior to eight or ten centuries back.

In matters of this kind, where there are little or no data to go on, any writer's opinion is open to argument, but still it is only by the writings of persons who have become acquainted with some of the tribes that any ethnological information can be collected. The writer of this has, in addition to the present work, brought out a Nága Grammar and an account of that people, and, in addition, an Historical Account of the Kacharis, a race formerly ruling Assam. In Burma, he trusts, to be able to gather valuable information regarding Shans and Kachyens.

C. A. SOPPITT.

BHAMO, BURMA:
*The 17th April 1887.*

# THE KUKI-LUSHAI TRIBES.

## CHAPTER I.—Physical Characteristics.

Population.

It is very difficult to ascertain exactly the number of souls in the various tribes and sub-tribes commonly spoken of as "Kukis," the only statistical records available being revenue returns, in which the number of houses alone is entered, and no mention made of the inmates.

The last census tables, those of 1881, embrace Kukis and Nágas under the one head, and it is impossible, therefore, to get any exact information from them. In the North Cachar Hills the Kuki population has been found to be (taking a certain number of houses, and striking an average of the inmates) about 20,000 and in the plains of Cachar 6,000. The Nága Hills district on the same calculation contains about 15,000 of the tribe, Manipur about 30,000 or 40,000, Tipperah 6,000.

The total of 77,000 or 87,000 thus arrived at is probably a little short of the actual number, but is, for all practical purposes, sufficiently correct. The Lushai tribes are not calculated.

Tribal designations.

The designation "Kuki" is unknown to the tribes now so-called by the plains people. What the derivation of the term may be it is hard to say. "Kou" in the language of the people now called "Lushais," and in the dialects of the Kuki tribes, signifies "a village."

The term "Lushai" can, in the opinion of the writer, be traced as regards it derivation. In some accounts of Burma mention is made of traces having been found of a people ruled over by the Lua kings or king, in days gone by. Now, in both dialects (Râng-khôl, &c.), the people ruled by the Lua king would be styled "Luahai," *i.e.*, "Lua people." This "Luahai" is almost identical with the term "Luashai," or "Lushai." This derivation, if the true one, is most important, and enables us to trace back the people for many ages, and into a country removed from the north-east frontier of India. The term "Kuki" might be traced in much the same manner, though the derivation may be considered, perhaps, less satisfactory than in the former case.

The Lushai people have only been known to us within comparatively recent years, and from the time of our first making their acquaintance, the intercourse between them and the plains ruled over by us has steadily increased. Their tribal designation has, therefore, but little changed when used in the dialects of the plains people, "Luahai" and "Lushai" being practically the same.

With the people commonly called "Kuki" the case is not the same. They occupied the borders long previous to the establishment of our rule, and their visits to the plains were few and far between. The name they styled themselves by was probably given to the few traders they came across as "Luahai," but the general plains population never saw them, and could only ascertain their name from those few traders. It is but natural that these men should change the name in repeating it to their own people, and that "Luahai" would first become "Lukai," then "Kukai," and ultimately "Kuki." A mistake of this sort is soon perpetrated when the people styled are rarely met with, and an error in the pronunciation cannot be corrected by them.

In the "Life of the Lindsays" mention is made of a tribe, living in the depths of the jungle, called "Cookies." At that date they were evidently looked upon as wild men of the woods, reference being made to one who was captured but afterwards succeeded in escaping to the woods, much in the same manner as a strange species of wild animal would be spoken of.

The designation "Kuki" is never used by the tribes themselves, though many of them answer to it when addressed, from knowing it to be the Bengali or plains term for their people. Neither do the Kacharis or Kachacha Nágas use the word; in the former language "Dakinsarao" being the name, and in the latter "Langtamê."

Tribal sects and divisions.

The so-called Kukis may be divided into four tribes:—

(1) Râangkhol.
(2) Bêtê.
(3) Jansên.
(4) Tadoï.

These terms are used by the villagers, and are their tribal designations in their own respective dialects. Each tribe, again, has another name for the other; thus, a Rângkhol speaking of No. (3) does not talk of a "Jansên," but calls him a "Kujon," and so on.

Some of these four sects or sub-tribes are sub-divided into minor divisions: thus, from the Rângkhols may be said to have sprung "Sakajaib" and "Kêlma" Kukis. These are, however, merely sub-divisions of the same, and it is simpler to speak of the four sects only.

It would perhaps be advisable to speak of these four as the four sub-tribes of a main race existing in former years in the country known to us as Lushai-land.

These four sub-tribes differ in customs, manners, and dialects to a certain extent, but have so much in common that there can be no doubt they originally belonged to one main tribe.

Among these four, again, some bear a closer affinity in speech and customs to one another than the others: thus, the Rangkol and Bêtê; the Jansen and Tadoï; and it might be almost justifiable to classify them in this manner:—

| | |
|---|---|
| (1) Rangkol, co-tribe Bêtê—offshoots | Sakajaib, Langrong. |
| (2) Jansen, co-tribe Tadoï—offshoots | Kotang, Shîk Shinshum, Râltê. |

The Langrongs are the Kukis inhabiting the Tipperah Hills, and are identical with the Rangkols. The Sakajaibs inhabit the North Cachar Hills Among the Jansen offshoots are placed the Râltês. These people have only very lately come from Lushai-land, and there are no great number of them in British territory. In Cachar (in a village near Nemotha) they are commonly spoken of, and looked upon, as Lushais. They may, perhaps, be looked upon as being the link between the real Lushais and the people now called Kukis.

Of the three tribes of Kukis inhabiting Manipur (Gôm, Kolrew, Sêri), the first two might be classified under the Rangkol head, and the last (Sêri) with the Jansens. The writer unfortunately has not had the same personal acquaintance with these four tribes as he has had with the others, and has had, therefore, to trust a great deal to hearsay. It is most important to avoid treating families or clans of the same people as separate sects or sub-tribes, and yet it is a mistake very easily made by anyone treating of a people with whose language he is not acquainted. An example will best illustrate the facility with which an error of the sort can be perpetrated. The hill Kacharis are all of one race, and call themselves "Dimâsârao," "the people of the great water:" yet in speaking among themselves, and in answering a question regarding the sub-divisions of the tribe, they are very apt to name several different kinds of Kacharis, as they put it: thus, "Saymsârao," "Asimsarao," "Sairsarao." These names signify "salt people," "Assam people," "iron people," and are not sub-tribes or even clans, but merely families of the "Dimâsârao," who in the old days (as regards 1 and 3) were told off by the Rája for certain duties, *i.e.*, salt and iron manufacture. A writer unacquainted with the language would be very apt, however, to classify the families as sub-tribes or clans.

In Hill Tipperah there are three tribes, named Paitu, Omroi, Korêng, all nearly connected with the Lushais. They might, perhaps, be classified with the Lushai as sub-tribes, and with them, perhaps, might be placed the Râltês, though it remains an open question as to whether this latter tribe should not remain with the Jansens. The writer's knowledge of the principal Kuki language, has, he trusts, enabled him to name the tribes and sub-tribes of the people, and not to confuse them with mere clans of one and the same sect.

In remarks under "origin" further reasons will be assigned for this.

Physique and character.

The Kukis generally are not as fine men as either the Angámi Nágas or the Kacharis, though many of them are sturdily built. They are short and squat as a rule, with high cheekbones and flat noses. Well-cut features are rarely met with, and their appearance, on the whole, is very effeminate. Little or no hair is grown on the face.

In character they are not nearly as honest as the Kachacha Nágas, though more so than the hill Kacharis, among which latter people lying is looked upon as a science worthy of every man's study, and deceit and deception are instilled into the child at the mother's breast. The Kukis are not a cheerful race, and cleanliness is far from being looked upon as a virtue. In hue the people are a darker brown than their neighbours, the Nágas; but their true colour is rarely seen, owing to the thick coating of dirt it is considered fashionable to wear. Among the four tribes, the Rangkols are by far the best specimens of mankind, being more cleanly and physically better made. Neither the men nor the women are at all handsome as a rule, the latter, in fact, when past a certain age, becoming repulsively ugly.

There is no authenticated case on record of a hill Kuki having been seen of his own free will indulging in a bath.

In former years the Kukis are reported to have rendered good service to Government in levies raised among the tribes. Nothing definite, however, can be pointed out as having been done by them, beyond the capture of a few villages, small ones, in which the odds were fifteen to one in favour of the attacking party.

Well armed by Government, and backed up by sepoys, they may have been of use in fights when anything was in their favour, but the experience of the writer, who has lived among them for some years, and is acquainted with their language, would lead him to place them low down in the scale as regards courage.

A militia of 100 strong was raised in the North Cachar Hills in 1880 after the Nága expedition for patrol and other purposes. A portion of the force (entirely Kuki) was engaged in a fight at Maibong against some hill Kacharis who had risen; but, instead of exhibiting valour, bolted to a man, leaving the sepoys of the Frontier Police to do the fighting.

Because the Kukis, backed up and armed by Government, have proved themselves on one or two occasions stronger than a few small bodies of their neighbours unarmed, comparatively speaking, an idea seems to prevail that the race is a warlike one.

Morality.

The morality of the Kukis, from a European point of view, is not by any means above being questioned. Among the Kachcha Nágas free intercourse is allowed between the youths and maidens in a village before marriage, though any breach of the marriage vows is severely dealt with. Among the Kukis more restrictions are placed on the actions of the young women of the community, a fine being inflicted on any man known to have formed a *liaison* with any one of the girls. At the same time, provided there be not too much publicity given to the love affairs, the maidens and youths are left a good deal to themselves. Further remarks on this subject will be found in the chapter on marriage.

Dress.

5. The Jansen and Tadoi Kukis (males) wear a strip of cloth, tied round the waist and falling down in front to about a foot or more above the knee. Nothing is worn behind. Earrings are some-

times used, and a few beads round the neck. *Pagris* are often seen.

Each man, in addition, when in the village, carries a loose cloth, used as a shawl. Very often, especially in unfrequented villages off the beaten tracks, the Jansen and Tadoï males go about entirely naked, with the exception of the shawl thrown over the shoulders.

The Rangkol and Bêtê males wear a strip of cloth tied round the waist, hanging both in front and behind. Beads are worn round the neck and large round earrings in the ears. They never appear naked.

The women in all four tribes wear a kilt of blue cloth, extending from the waist to just above the knee, and another cloth from the breasts to the waist.

Bracelets and earrings are worn in great profusion.

The hair among male and female Rangkols is drawn back, and tied in a knot at the back of the head. Occasionally, long brass hair-pins are fastened in.

The Bêtê, Tadoï, and Jansen men wear their hair in the same way, but the women plait it before fastening it at the back of the head.

Many of the Kuki women, on marrying and taking to the serious business of life,—cutting fire-wood and slaving in the *jhúms* (paddy-fields),—give up their ornaments.

Arms.

The original Kuki arms were bows and arrows and a long sword-like weapon made of iron; but for very many years guns of some sort have been in use, and at the present day a bow is never seen. The ordinary every-day arm now is a spear and *dao*.

## CHAPTER II.— Habits and Religion.

Origin.

The actual origin of the four tribes, Rangkol, Bêtê, Jansen, Tadoï, commonly spoken of as "the Kukis," is very obscure.

That they formerly occupied the country we call Lushai-land is known, and their movements, since leaving those hills, can be traced; but previous to that nothing is certain. In common with all the hill tribes bordering Assam, the very early history of the Kukis will in all probability remain unwritten, though the different grammars and vocabularies being compiled of late years may possibly lead link by link to the tracing of many, now, apparently totally distinct tribes, back to a common stock.

A great deal of the later history of these tribes can be made out, and, from what has already occurred, a fair opinion can be formed of the movements now going on, at a considerable distance inland from our frontier, it is true, but still important to us as pointing to a time when we shall be brought into contact with the promoters of these movements.

About the middle of the sixteenth century, as near as can be ascertained, the Rangkols (Kukis) inhabited the country now occupied by the Lushais, bordering Cachar, and their neighbourrs were the Bêtês (Kukis), with whom they were on friendly terms and whose language and their own was practically the same. In other words, the Bêtês were a co-tribe, though not one and the same.

The present Jansens (Kukis) lived in the hills immediately at the back of the Rangkols, and commenced to oppress them; by degrees succeeding in driving them nearer and nearer the plains, and then ultimately out of the country across Cachar into the North Cachar Hills and Manipur, a small body taking refuge in Tipperah territory. Scarcely had the Rangkols been driven out, when the Bêtês found themselves in much the same position as regards the oppression exercised by the Jansens, and, following in the footsteps of their friends (the Rangkols), crossed into Cachar.

We thus find the Rangkols and their co-tribe, the Bêtês, driven out of Lushai-land (now so-called), not by the people called Lushais, though they may or may not have indirectly aided the exodus, but by the Jansens (Kukis).

The Jansens, or, to make things plainer, the Jansen Kukis, now found themselves occupying the Cachar frontier with their neighbours, the Tadoïs (Kukis), with whom they were on friendly terms, and who bore the same relation to them as the Bêtês did to the Rangkols. These Tadoïs benefited by the conquest and expulsion of the Rangkols, and probably aided, to a small extent, their friends.

Immediately at the back of the Jansens and their co-tribe, the Tadoïs, were settled the Lushais (the people now so-called), who were gradually extending from further back towards Cachar (north).

These Lushais soon began to make their power felt, and, after struggling for many years in vain, the Jansens and Tadoïs were driven out, and found themselves following in the footsteps of their conquered foes, the Rangkols. This second exodus (the Jansen-Tadoï) took place about the earlier part of the present century.

We thus see the Rangkol (Kukis), with a co-tribe, the Bêtê (Kukis), driven out by a tribe, named the Jansens (Kukis), and their co-tribe, the Tadoï (Kukis); the conquerors (the Jansens) being, with the co-tribe Tadoï, in their turn driven out by the people known to us as the Lushais.

The four tribes are commonly spoken of as "Kukis" and are regarded as being one and the same, the only distinction made, as a rule, being that one body is stated to have been forced across the plains a considerable time previous to the expulsion of the other. In official documents the distinction between the two bodies is made by calling one the "old Kukis" in counterdistinction to the others, the "new Kukis," but no mention is made of the fact that they are as distinct as the Lushais, and the people now at their back the Poeys, though both these latter tribes must have a great deal in common.

We now see the Lushais slowly being pressed forward by the Poeys, and there can be no reasonable doubt that in a few years Cachar will again become the refuge of the conquered (some Lushais have settled already in British territory), and while the Lushais settle about the North Cachar Hills, the Poeys will remain in their place on our frontier supreme, until, in their turn, ousted by tribes of which we as yet know nothing.

The great stumbling-block has been the term "Kuki," applied indiscriminately to four sub-tribes who should have retained their regular appellations, Rangkol, Bêtê, Jansen, and Tadoï; or, at any rate, the two main tribes should have been kept distinct (Rangkols and Jansens), and the terms "old" and "new" Kukis not have been used.

In the grammar attached, it will be seen that the difference in language is as considerable between the Rangkols and Jansens as it is between the Rangkols and Lushais.

The whole six tribes or sub-tribes, Rangkols, Bêtê, Jansen, Tadoï, Lushai, Poey, or, not to sub-divide a race more than possible, the four tribes,—

(1) Rangkols, co-tribe Bêtê,
(2) Jansens, ditto Tadoï,
(3) Lushais,
(4) Poeys,

came doubtless from one common stock, and might therefore be spoken of with a common tribal affix in addition to their ordinary designation, though it would be hard, indeed, to settle on the affix. Failing this, they must bear their sub-tribal names, and cannot be subjected to an arbitrary grouping in the way the Rangkols and Jansens have been, with their co-tribes, under the head of "Kuki." This distinction has been maintained in the case of Nágas: thus, we have Kachcha Nágas, Angámi Nágas, Kowpoi Nágas, &c.

Many of the Kukis (so-called), after being driven from Lushai-land, settled not only in the North Cachar Hills, but extended on into the Nága Hills district and into Manipur territory, where they remain to the present day.

The first settlers in the North Cachar Hills, then under the Kachari "Raj," paid tribute regularly to the Rája at Maibong; but they do not appear to have been otherwise interfered with by the Kacharis, with whom they lived on the best of terms.

Mode of building.

All the Kukis build the same kind of house as is constructed by the people we call the Lushais. A raised platform, about 3 or 4 feet from the ground, is first put up, and on this an ordinary hut erected, and the roof thatched with grass or cane leaves. In front of the main entrance, a space is left for a verandah. The interior of the house is partitioned off into two, three, and sometimes more rooms, according to the number of inmates.

The villages are situated on hill tops, or on ridges, the houses facing one another, with a broad path running down the centre.

Drink and food.

The common drink is distilled from rice, and, when new, is very intoxicating, gradually becoming less and less powerful the longer it is kept. In colour it somewhat resembles dark brandy. On the occasion of funeral ceremonies and other events when feasts are held, large quantities of the liquor are consumed.

As regards food, very little comes amiss to a Kuki. Tigers and leopards are not eaten by any of the tribes, and dogs by the Bêtês only.

Monkeys are considered a great delicacy by all, except the Tadoïs and Rangkols, whose palates have not apparently been educated up to that point. With the exception of a Rangkol, any Kuki will rejoice greatly at the capture of a python, and a cheerful and animated appearance extends itself gradually over his face, as he measures off his captive, and calculates the number of his friends he can comfortably entertain on the flesh.

The Rangkhol, owing to a certain fastidiousness, is again out of it when a fat bamboo rat is the object of search. Though either a Bêtê, Jansen, or Tadoï will show unwonted energy at the mere sight of the animal, and will scramble hurriedly down the steepest of steep places in order to effect a capture, he will gaze unmoved at the hunt, and even when the prey is brought up and ocular demonstration (by sundry punches in the rat's ribs) given that it is fat, will still remain unconcerned. Let, however, a porcupine or ant-eater cross his path, and with one war-whoop he puts himself on the track, and the stoical reserve hitherto maintained is abandoned. Even the body of a deer or pig found in the jungles, alive with maggots, is not despised, maggots being considered rather a delicacy than otherwise by all the tribes.

As might be expected; where the Kukis have been brought into close relations with more civilised people, they have abandoned many of their former articles of food.

Many a semi-plains Kuki will scorn a monkey, though his mouth waters as he watches one of his hill brothers, as yet unsophisticated and natural, sitting down and making elaborate preparations for the cooking thereof.

Caste.

There is no caste, strictly speaking, among any of the tribes. As already mentioned, some of the people give up eating certain things on living near plains people, but this is simply because they are laughed or sneered at by them, and for no other reason. Cows are not kept, nor is the flesh eaten, but the wild ox (*Bos frontalis*), termed "mithun" (some of which are kept in a domesticated state by all villages), is slaughtered for the purposes of food, and is greedily partaken of by all.

Smoking.

The Rangkols seldom smoke, but Jansens and Tadoïs are rarely seen without a pipe in their mouth. Rájas, and headman generally, keep a certain number of women employed every day and all day in smoking tobacco and collecting the juice. The pipe used for this purpose bears a resemblance to an ordinary clay pipe stuck on end into a small round bamboo box, to the middle of which box a mouthpiece is attached at an acute angle. The box is half filled with water, and the juice running down the stem of the clay falls into it. Each day this mixture is poured out into a small gourd the Raja carries about his person. A sip is occasionally taken. On the meeting of two Rájas their respective bottles are exchanged, a mouthful of the contents swallowed, and the bottles returned.

Rice: method of planting.

The staple food is rice, grown on the hill sides round about the villages. The land chosen is cleared, the jungle being cut and allowed to dry, preparatory to burning, in March and April or earlier. At the end of April and the commencement of May it is burned clear. With a hoe the surface is then slightly scraped, and the rice sown. Even the very steepest of hill sides are cut for *jhúming* purposes, the rainfall being sufficient to mature hill rice without artificial aid. The crop is cut about the end of October ; but the time both for planting and gathering differs slightly at higher or lower elevations. Good land is planted two or even three years in succession. As a rule, however, new *jhúms* are cut each season.

Religious belief.

The Rangkols believe in three principal gods,—Lambra, Golarai, and Dudukal.

Lambra is the head god or creator, and, without his consent, nothing can be done by the others. Golarai is the god of death. Dudukal causes sickness occasionally, but more often works for the good of mankind. When this latter god has to cause death, he carries out the decree through his wife Fapitê.

In sacrificing to Lambra, a goat and four fowls should be used, but it is allowable to dispense with the goat. The fowls may be of any colour. Two fowls and a goat are offered to Golarai and Dudukal.

There is no one particular god devoted to war. Benaiki is a minor god who keeps guard over all property. One fowl only is used in offering to him. Pigs are never used for sacrificial purposes. There are numerous minor deities working for good and evil, all more or less under the command of the head god, but their designations vary considerably in each locality, and they are not worthy of note. Sacrifices to Lambra are offered towards the rising sun; to Golarai at midday (as a rule) to the north; and to Dudukal in the evening to the south.

Method of sacrifice.

The following is the procedure in vogue at the larger sacrificial ceremonies :—

Two pieces of bamboo are stuck in the ground, and on to these a cross piece fastened. At the back of this erection, at the distance of a foot or more, are planted 10 smaller sticks in a line. The bird or animal to be killed is then brought to the rear of these sticks, and the throat cut or the head chopped off, the reason of the offering being at the same time stated. The heads of the animals used for sacrificial purposes are left on the spot, the bodies being taken away and cooked.

Ceremonies on death.

On the death of a man his spirit is believed to remain one full moon in the house he occupied when living, at the lapse of that time departing to a village termed "the village of the dead," where it stays until returned to earth (at the lapse of an uncertain number of years) in the body of a new-born child. Good and bad men go to the same village, but people carried off by tigers or killed by accident or in war, though still going there, live apart from the others. The gods do not inhabit the "village of the dead."

All "mithun," fowls, goats, &c., killed on the death of a man, accompany him in a future state.

On the decease of a man all the relatives and friends are assembled. The day after the death a large pile of crossed pieces of wood is raised in the jungle outside the village, and on this the body placed and more wood added. The nearest male bachelor relative of the deceased then stands on one side of the pyre, and sets light to it. As it burns he throws across small pieces of bamboo stem filled with water, calling out at the same time in the following terms—"Be as jungle: return to jungle." At the conclusion of the cremation, any bones left are collected, and, with the cooking utensils, &c., of the deceased, are placed in a miniature hut built on the spot. The friends and relatives then return to the village, and hold a feast. The morning following an offering is made to the gods.

Other belief.

The other Kuki tribes have much the same religious belief on the whole, though the head gods are differently named. In fact, in those of all the semi-savage tribes a great similarity is invariably found,—a head god, his assistants, other powerful deities, working for the good and evil of mankind, and their aids minor gods: means of propitiation, sacrifice. This similarity cannot be said to carry much weight in an argument in favour of the common origin, at no very remote date, of many of these tribes, for the reason that the beliefs and superstitions are those that would naturally be acquired by a people living in the same way more or less, in the same kind of country and subject to the same diseases, epidemical visitations, and calamities. It is far more probable that common origin is to be traced by the study of social manners, languages, traditionary legends, &c., than by religious belief. A tribe settling in a new country would soon change its belief, especially when that belief was a crude and more or less unformed one. Thus, removing to a part of a province where storms were unusually severe, as compared to what they were in the place from whence they came, a people would naturally adopt a "god of storms," which "god of storms" most probably was acknowledged by the original inhabitants of that part. In this way, a similarity in the religion of the two would spring up at once.

Jansen death ceremonies.

As regards ceremonies on death, a considerable difference exists in the different tribes. The Rangkols and a sect closely allied to them, in fact an offshoot, the Sakajaibs, burn their dead. The Bêtês, though of the same tribe, do not do so, but, in common with the Jansens and co-tribe Tadoïs, dispose of the dead by burial.

Jansen graves.

The grave is dug to a depth of four or five feet, and at the bottom on one side, in such a way that the body lies at right-angles to the main grave, is dug a hole sufficiently long to hold a coffin. In this niche the corpse, fastened down in the coffin, a rough box made of planks and sometimes of bamboos tied together, is placed, and the grave filled in with stones and earth. The head of the corpse faces west and the feet east, Over the grave poles are erected, and to them fastened the heads of the animals slaughtered for the funeral feast. As with the Rangkols, all spirits, whether they have committed good or bad actions in this world, are received in the "village of the dead;" but this proviso is made: should a person during life have injured any one or committed murder, his or her victim will meet the spirit on the road, and stop the path. A fight will then ensue, by which the spirit is purified, and then permitted to pass. The person injured by the deceased may, of course, be still living, in which case a spirit is appointed by the gods as a substitute. It is owing to this that dead persons are buried with their weapons of war, to be ready for the fray. There are certain ways by which a spirit can avoid having to fight persons he has injured in this life; one being by peace-offerings of pigs, goats, birds, &c. For this reason it is customary to place the heads of animals over graves. On meeting the injured spirit, one of the goats or pigs, as the case may be, accompanying deceased in a ghostly form, is offered, and, if accepted, the fight does not take place.

Death of Jansen Rája.

A strange and more or less disgusting custom exists among the Jansens and their co-tribe, the Tadoïs, as regards the disposal of the corpse of a Rája or any relative of a Rája's.* Immediately on

* NOTE.—The Rangkols and the co-tribe do not acknowledge Rájas.

the death becoming known, the whole community, and any relatives and friends living in other villages, are assembled, and mithun, goats, fowls, pigs, &c., slaughtered for a feast. Each funeral guest, if not a relative, is expected to give one cloth for the use of the corpse; if a relative, two, three, or more.

In these cloths the body is carefully wrapped, and at the end of a few days, sometimes at the lapse of a day, it is carried out and placed on a raised platform at a distance of 30 or 40 yards from the house. Here it is left to decompose. At the end of every three days the female relatives are obliged to visit the platform, or *machan*, and so fasten up the cloths (as decomposition sets in and is progressing) that none of the putrid matter falls to the ground. During the whole of this period general feasting is kept up at the expense of the deceased Rája, and only ceases when the supply of liquor runs short, or the corpse has thoroughly decomposed, and nothing is left but the skeleton. The bones and cloths are then carefully gathered, and buried in front of the house, but the skull is reserved for further ceremonies. It is first bleached in the sun, any loose teeth being refastened in with gum, and then, being thoroughly cleaned, it is placed in a woven cane basket. Another feast is now held, at the conclusion of which this basket is carefully hidden away by the relatives. During the earlier days, when decomposition has fairly set in, the stench in a village is fearful; but this is blunted somewhat to the anything but sensitive nostrils of the inhabitants by large fires kept burning day and night. It was formerly customary on the decease of a Rája to kill a certain number of persons, slaves or prisoners of war, and place their heads on the platform with the body. This custom exists still among the people we call "Lushais."

## CHAPTER III.—MARRIAGE AND INHERITANCE.

Rangkol laws.

In a manner, child marriage is allowed by the Rangkols though the custom is not very common Thus, a man may bespeak the newly-born daughter of another for himself or his son; but, until the girl is full grown, the couple are not allowed to live together. The preliminaries to an ordinary marriage are as follows:—A man having taken a fancy to a girl offers a present of liquor to the parents and talks the matter over. Should they be willing to accept him as a son-in-law, he takes up his abode with them for three years, working in the *jhúms*, and practically becoming a bond servant. At the end of this period he is allowed to marry the girl, but even then is not free, as he has to remain on another two seasons, working in the same manner as he did before. At the completion of the five years he is free to build a separate house and start life on his own account. Two rupees is the sum ordinarily paid the parents of the girl, a sum paid evidently more for the purpose of proving a contract than for anything else, the long period of servitude being the real price paid. A Kuki wife is rarely known to prove false to her husband. As already mentioned, a great deal of freedom is allowed to the maids and youths in a village; but once a husband has been chosen, the matter assumes a different aspect, any breach of the marriage vows being visited by fines purposely made so heavy that no ordinary villager can pay them, and is bound in consequence to serve as a slave to any person from whom he can borrow the amount required to make good the sum. The Jansens buy their wives, and do not serve a probationary period.

Illegitimate children.

It not uncommonly happens, as a result of the intercourse allowed between the maids and youths in a community, that some of the girls become mothers without going through the ceremony constituting marriage. When this occurs, the father is fined a small amount if he states his willingness to marry the girl, but a larger amount if he refuses to have anything to say to her. In the latter event, the child remains with the mother, but should she marry afterwards is made over to her relatives. No particular slur is cast upon a person born out of wedlock.

Divorce.

Once married, no divorce is allowed except for adultery, and even in these cases, if there be children, it is rarely resorted to. The adulterer is heavily fined, but does not otherwise suffer punishment.

Number of wives.

A man is allowed one wife only. A Jansen is allowed three wives. The first wife (should a second one be brought to the house) is obliged by custom to rush at the bride and strip her naked. This is done to put the new comer to shame, and thus maintain the supremacy of the first wife, whose modesty has not been outraged.

Deceased brother's wife.

A man, if not already married, is bound to marry the widow of a deceased elder brother. Even if he be a mere child, he will, on coming of age, marry the woman, however old she may be.

An elder brother may not marry the widow of the younger. A man may marry his wife's younger sister, but not the elder.

Rights of succession.

Only male children can inherit property. In the event of several, the eldest son gets all, and is at liberty to distribute or not to his younger brothers. Girls are sometimes allowed to retain a small portion of any jewellery belonging to the mother, but that is all.

In the event of wife being divorced, &c.

In the event of a wife being divorced, leaving male children with the father, and the man re-marrying, and having other male progeny, the boys of both families inherit equally.

Only girls.

Should a man have daughters only, and no sons, the property passes to the nearest male relative of the deceased, the daughters receiving nothing.

On the death of husband.

On the death of a husband with no children, or with only girls and no sons, the property does not remain with the widow, but passes, as in the above case, to the nearest male relative of the deceased.

Widows and widowers.

On the death of a wife the widower is not permitted to remarry within the period of three years, but, on the other hand, a widow is at liberty to remarry at once.

Naming of children.

On the birth of a child the name to be given is settled upon, not by the parents, but by the elders of the community. Subsequent to the birth, the father and mother drop their own names, and are addressed by that borne by their offspring, the terms for father and mother being affixed: thus, "so-and-so's father," "so-and-so's mother." Should a couple grow old and have no issue, they are addressed as "the childless father," "the childless mother."

Jansen and Tadoi laws.

The Jansens purchase their wives. The price to be paid for the girl having been settled by the bridegroom elect during the course of two visits, and the money made over, the following ceremony takes place. The bride and bridegroom sit on the ground, the hojai, or priest, standing over them, holding a fowl by the neck. From the contortions the bird's body goes through while being slowly strangled, the priest judges whether the marriage will be a happy one or not. Next, a glass of liquor is handed to the husband, who drinks half, and gives the rest to his wife. The priest then cuts off the wings of the fowl, placing the right one in the man's hair and the left in the woman's. The marriage is now complete.

Royal marriages.

A separate procedure is adopted on the marriage of the daughters of Rájas. A suitor having presented himself (preliminary arrangements being settled as regards the amount to be paid), his courage and perseverance are tested in the following manner:—A leg of pork is hung up inside a house, and all the female inhabitants of the village are assembled, each armed with a strip of cloth, to the end of which is fastened a bag of stones. These women, of all ages, from the girl of seven to the venerable hag of eighty summers, then place themselves round about the house in such a way that any one attempting to approach must pass by them. The would-be wooer is now told to try and take away the piece of meat hanging inside. On a given signal, he makes a rush, which the women endeavour to frustrate by striking him with the slings in their hands. Should he succeed in his object, he is again mercilessly treated on re-appearing from the house, and is chased through the village out into the jungle.

If the piece of meat is dropped, the beating ceases and the man is loudly laughed at, and told that he is not good enough for the girl, and had better return from whence he came.

Should he succeed in getting clear of the village, his companions, whom he has brought for the purpose, quietly take possession of the girl, and remove her unmolested.

An ordinary villager cannot aspire to the hand of a Rája's daughter, it being necessary that the suitor should be a blood relation to some other Rája.

## CHAPTER IV.—Government of Villages.

Internal government of villages and sects.

In treating of the internal government of these tribes, the justice of classifying the people, now generally known as Kukis, under the two heads "Rangkol, co-tribe Bêtê," and Jansen, co-tribe "Tadoï" (the others falling under the one or the other head), will be at once seen.

Rangkol Government.

The Rangkols and the sects allied to them recognize no Rájas, each village being ruled by a "galim" (headman), aided by a "gabur" (assistant headman), and two subordinates, a "chapiah galim" and "chapiah gabur"—Their titles are not hereditary.

On the death of a "galim," the "gabur" is raised to his place, and so on; thus a man, before he can become a "galim," has to work up through all the grades from "chapiah gabur."

Each community is separate, and stands by itself, having nothing to do with any other as regards internal management.

The different positions from galim down carry certain privileges, the holders having no coolie work to do, for example. It is customary to distribute all fines levied on private individuals among the fellow villagers, the "galims," &c., receiving large shares, and being in this way pecuniarily remunerated for their services.

The "galim" is president of all village councils, and has, with his subordinates, a great deal of the say in any matter affecting the community. All village disputes, quarrels, fights, &c., are brought up to him, and a decision arrived at by him with the help of as many as care to gather round and express their opinions. In the old days this decision was seldom questioned, but it is now frequently appealed to the nearest magistrate. Each village has one "galim" only, and not two or three.

Priests.

There are several priests in each community who settle the time and duration of *pujas*, &c. These men are chosen for some apparent fitness, such as their own statements that they are subject to visions and visitations from gods, and the appointments are not hereditary. The principal duty of the priest is in offering sacrifices to the deities, appeasing the evil-inclined ones on the occasions of sickness, and propitiating the well-disposed at the time of rice-planting, &c. The priests are remunerated by the present of one cloth per annum from each house and a little rice; but should they visit another village, they are allowed to charge one rupee and a cloth for each occasion of sacrifice.

Jansen government.

The Jansens and sects allied to them are governed by Rájas. Sometimes a group of villages is ruled over by one, or, as is more frequently the case, each community has it own. Each Rája has a mantri (minister) to aid him.

The government was despotic,* and in the hands of the Rája were the lives of the people. His decision was final in all matters, and was never questioned. At the present day (putting aside heinous crime, which is dealt with by Government), he has practically the whole say in anything affecting the welfare of the village or villages under his rule.

On each house is levied a tax of one basket (about ¾md.) of rice per annum for the use of the royal household. In addition, of any litter of pigs one is given to the Rája, and in the same way one leg of anything shot is presented. It will be seen that there is a considerable difference in the methods of internal government of these two tribes, Rangkols and Jansens, and their respective co-tribes and sects. The difference is so marked that there can be no hesitation in classifying the tribes, co-tribes, and sects accordingly. It is true, the Rangkols have an old legend among them that ages ago they were ruled over by a king, "arêng," but there is no trustworthy information on the subject. At any rate, the truth or otherwise of the legend does not to any appreciable extent affect the question, as the Jansen Rájas' positions, as at present found, are hereditary, with well-defined rights, powers, and duties, and are evidently not the creations of late years. It is true that, allowing the Rangkols and Jansens to have been one and the same race at *no remote date*, under one head or Rája, on separation the two sects might have adopted different customs; but it would be difficult to account for the great dissimilarity, the despotic rule on the one hand, as viewed against the self government on the other.

This is pointed out merely to support the argument that the Rangkols and Jansens (commonly considered one tribe, and called Kukis) are as distinct, and should be kept as distinct, from one another as the people now called the Lushais are kept from either of them, and it is not contended that there was no *remote* common origin, for, as already mentioned, the common origin is placed almost beyond doubt by the similarity to be found in the dialects.

Pujas and festivals.

On the occasions of general *pujas* the entrances to all Kuki villages are closed, and no outsider allowed to enter. On ordinary festivals the village is open to all.

* In the old days, at present, of course, the Jansens and others are subject to British rule.

Method of waging war.

Before settling on an attack, the gods are consulted to ascertain whether the omens are propitious or not. One of the priests holds up a fowl, while another chops off the head. On the position in which the head falls depends the success or otherwise of the expedition. Should the beak face towards the village to be attacked, the omen is a good one; should it fall in the opposite direction a sign of the defeat of the party; while should it point to the priest, it foretells the total annihilation of any attacking force.

The omens being favourable, the attacking party start off, led by a warrior of some renown. The attack takes place either at night or at daybreak, and generally ceases when the sun is fairly up.

Heads of foe.

The heads of the foe slain are brought back by the victors, or, should these be too numerous, the ears alone are preserved. A war dance is held round the trophies, which are planted about the village on poles. Prisoners are never taken. A warrior getting a head is obliged to pay ten rupees to the elder brother of his mother as a sort of thanksgiving for his success. Women and children, as well as men, are killed in war.

Dancing.

Dancing is one of the principal amusements in a Kuki village. These dances are of many kinds, all of which, though more or less interesting, are not worthy of any special description. Music is supplied by a species of reed instrument, and time kept to the striking of bamboos on the ground. Among the dances for males alone the following are described as being typical.

*The crossed bamboo dance.*—In this two men, holding the ends of bamboos in each hand, sit facing one another. Two others then place themselves, so that the bamboos which they hold in the same way cross at right-angles those held by the others. The two sets of men then alternatively bring their bamboos sharply together, and as quickly back again to their original position on the either side of their body. By this means a number of squares are formed and reformed. A youth then advances, and is expected to spring in and out of the squares, without being struck by the bamboos, keeping time to the music, which gradually grows faster and faster. The bamboos are brought backwards and forwards to the same tune, and the dancer has to be very quick indeed to avoid being caught in one or other of the squares, to say nothing of the unpleasantness of being struck with the bamboos on the shin.

The tiger dance is another popular one. A cloth done up to represent a pig or a goat is placed on the ground, and one of the youths of the village proceeds to imitate a tiger stalking it. The attitudes assumed are most amusing, and it is wonderful how some of the men, while on all fours, spring over the imaginary goat and alight on the other side.

Jumping.

Jumping is another source of amusement in a village; high jumping being that most generally indulged in. Two bamboos tied together are first held up, and then gradually drawn further and further apart, the object being to jump as wide, as well as high, as possible. An extraordinary custom exists among the Kachcha Nágas as regards winners: they having to give, in lieu of receiving, a prize. Thus, on the conclusion of a contest between two villages, the leaders of the losing side seize the winner, and either strip him, his clothes becoming their property, or make him give them a present. This custom does not exist among the Kukis, the winner receiving the prize, whatever it may be.

The Nága argument is that a man finding himself a winner, and therefore, in that particular line, superior to others, should be thankful and willing to pay for his good fortune.

## CHAPTER V.—Crimes and Oaths.

Crimes how punished.

All crimes, even the most serious, appear to have been punished by fine only, and are now (in independent territory) punished by fine only.

Form of oath.

On the occasion of any oath being taken, either on the restoration of peace between villages or between private individuals, the following is the procedure:—

A bear's or tiger's skull is placed upon the ground, a nettle-leaf, husk (paddy), and a sword blade. The persons (or person) to be sworn then step forward, and repeat the terms of the treaty or agreement, and, pointing to the skull, say—"If I break faith, may a bear or tiger, similar to the one this skull belonged to, devour me; may I be stung by the nettle now before me; may the seed I sow be as fruitless as this husk; and may I be struck by a sword. Heaven and earth now witness this oath."

Test of veracity.

There is one very strange custom in force among all the Kukis for testing the truth of a man's words. It being impossible to ascertain the respective veracity of two statements, the parties interested agree to appeal to the water-test. All the villagers are assembled, and proceed to some spot on a river where the water is deep. Here two bamboos are fixed firmly in the mud or gravel at the bottom. The priest of the village then cuts the throat of a white fowl on the brow of each disputant, allowing the blood to run down the face. Should the blood flow red in one case and blackish in the other, the matter is considered half proved, the red showing the man whose statement was true. To make matters certain the test has to be completed. At a given signal, both men plunge into the river, and, by the aid of the bamboos, attempt to get to the bottom, and bring up some mud or a stone. The one who fails is the guilty party. This test is considered infallible by the Kukis, who maintain that the very best swimmer, if in the wrong, can never reach the bottom, however desperately he may attempt to do so.

Occasionally, neither party succeeds in bringing up mud or stones, and in this case both are considered to have been in the wrong.

## CHAPTER VI.—Miscellaneous.

Relations with other tribes.

There are no cases on record of any of the various Kuki sects having raided on either Kachári or Nága villages, and their relations with these and neighbouring tribes appear to have been invariably of a friendly nature. The Rangkol settlers in the North Cachar Hills paid revenue to the Kachári Rája during the period of that dynasty in North Cachar, but were not otherwise troubled.

Land disputes.

Land disputes are very rare, owing to the large area available for cultivation in the vicinity of most of the settlements, and the scant populations generally; one village having no reason to encroach on the grounds of another.

In former years, when disputes did arise, might was right, and the stronger held the land.

Trade and manufacture.

Very little in the way of manufacturing articles is done by the Kukis. The women weave a few rough cotton cloths, which are afterwards dyed blue, the dye being obtained from a species of dwarf indigo grown near the villages. Iron, in the shape of *dao* blades, is imported from the plains.

"Mithun," the wild ox (*bos frontalis*), are kept in a domesticated state in all the villages. They are kept for trading and festival purposes, and are never milked. The domesticated animal resembles the wild species in every respect, with the one exception of the horns, those of the former being straight and cowlike, while those of the latter are curved. Though allowed to wander free in the jungles, the herds are perfectly tame, and show no fear of a European. The price for a full-grown "mithun" varies from 40 to 80 rupees. Among the people the value of property is often spoken of as so many "mithun;" in this case a "mithun" being equivalent to 40 rupees. A Rája, for example, will say he gave so many "mithun" for his wife, meaning so many 40 rupees.

Very little is done in the way of trade. In common with most hill tribes, the Kuki has few wants. A small patch of forest, cleared and sown with paddy, keeps him in rice throughout the year; his wife weaves the few cloths he requires in the way of clothing, and the neighbouring jungles keep him supplied with innumerable wild yams and herbs generally, besides occasionally affording him a treat in the shape of venison or pork.

The only necessary he has to purchase is salt, and this he can get a sufficiency of by selling wax gathered in the jungle or a maund of cotton. Dhal and ghee have no charms for him, and so he does not care to purchase them. He thus has no need of money. As civilization advances trade increases, simply for the reason that expensive tastes are acquired, and the hitherto unsophisticated Kuki, content to wander about with little or no clothing, finds it suddenly necessary to array himself in cloths of many colours; perhaps even his skull, hitherto impregnable to the rays of the sun, appears to him to be more susceptible than formerly, necessitating, in consequence, the use of an umbrella to shade it. He gets a liking for ghee or oil, and begins to look upon dhal as a necessity, while the fatted pup or bamboo rat he once relished appears no longer to be the dainty fare it did. To gratify his tastes he must have money, and to get money he must trade.

The wife soon wakes to the change which has come over her lord and master, and finds she has more work than ever in the cotton fields; that she has to plant chillies and innumerable other marketable produce, in addition to what had been formerly grown. She finds, moreover, that the excess loads necessitate her aiding to carry them to the plains, or the nearest bázár, and so she joins her husband, and is brought, as he was, to see and appreciate the advantages of civilization, as illustrated by ghee, sugar, and other luxuries. In exchange for the tastes they acquire, they lose all their simple and confiding nature. The plausible trader from whom they buy has opened their eyes to the wiles and deceptions practised in civilized society; to hold their own they must deceive, and so they lose sight of that primitive but more or less honest way of dealing they have been brought up to, and become rather more thoroughpaced liars than their teacher.

Their old code of morality was strictly adhered to. The intercourse of youths and maidens before marriage was by it not much restricted, it is true, but such a thing as a man having taken unto himself a wife, then proving untrue, had been a crime scarcely conceivable to them, and so rarely heard of as almost to be said not to exist.

Now, the man sees men married like himself indulging in vice more or less openly, and it suddenly breaks upon him that a simple, honest, industrious life is not at all the thing, and he consequently plunges rather more wildly into dissipation than an ordinary plainsman would do.

It may be said that the first step towards civilization is a total demoralization of the hillman. He spurns his own code of morality and social laws generally, simply from seeing how these laws are despised by people far more numerous and powerful than his own, and is looked upon in consequence as more or less of an outcast by his own tribe and by all others. Further contact with the people of the plains results in the adoption of some form or other of Hinduism, and with it new manners and customs. He then commences to regain the self respect he has lost, and becomes in the course of time a respectable member of society. He cannot, however, avoid the period he has to remain an outcast. The customs of his own people he has broken through, and they will have nothing to say to him, while those of his own kind who have already embraced Hinduism look down upon him.

Cotton.

Cotton is grown in the hills to a small extent. The crop is planted in March and April, appears above ground in June, and is gathered in November and December. The price per maund (uncleaned cotton) varies from Rs. 4 to Rs. 5. Cotton from which the seeds have been extracted is far more expensive.

The silkworm is not kept by the Kukis.

## CHAPTER VII.—TRAPS AND SNARES.

In late years the Kukis have obtained a comparatively large number of guns, and have in consequence lost a great deal of their skill is setting traps for game. Still, even now in favourite localities round about the villages traps of different kinds are set. The principal ones are the "gâslê" and "kûr."

The former is set in the following manner:—A deer or other run, passing down a steep bank, is chosen, and on the slope are placed small whole bamboos, side by side. These are covered with dry bamboo leaves. At the foot of the bamboo, sharpened sticks are placed in the ground, the points facing towards the slope.

An animal trying to get down the bank slips on the bamboos, and, before it can recover itself, is impaled on the spears at the bottom. When this trap is set, its whereabouts is made known to all the villagers, as it is most dangerous to human life. All kinds of animals, from tigers to small deer and porcupine, are destroyed by it.

The "kûr" is another trap dangerous to sportsmen and people wandering in the jungles unacquainted with the locality. A natural-looking fence is thrown up along a mile or two of country. This fence is made of dried sticks, and is so constructed that, though it offers considerable impediment to progress, it is so frail as to almost appear as though formed from branches blown down from the trees. Gaps are left here and there in this hedge; alongside each gap a spear being tied to a sapling in such a manner that on a catch, fastened to a creeper passing across the path, being released, the spear flies across. A sportsman, seeing this apparently natural fence, is very apt, in preference to alarming game by breaking through the dead branches, to walk down the side until he finds a gap.

The common pitfalls are too well known to need description; there is, however, one other snare worthy of notice.

A young tree is bent down to the side of a path, across which a big noose is laid. The end of the noose is fastened to the tree, and is so arranged that an animal passing releases the sapling, and is suspended by a fore or hind leg some 10 or 15 feet from the ground.

A story is told of two sepoys of the Frontier Police who had been told off to take an important dâk during one of the many Nâga expeditions. One of the men had lingered behind his companion in some village, and on following him later came upon his rifle lying on the path. He first thought of tigers, but one look at the ground showed there had been no struggle. He then hunted about some time, and at last was attracted by a moaning sound overhead. When, on looking up, he beheld to his astonishment his companion hanging by the leg to a tree. Luckily, the man had succeeded in slightly drawing himself up by holding on to his thigh, and so kept the blood from running to the head, but he was so exhausted from former shouting that he could only moan. He was soon cut down, but there is nothing on record to show that he was afterwards particularly anxious to march along jungle paths without a guide.

The heights of different animals are calculated in the following manner:—

An elephant, three times the diameter of the footprint, or, roughly, one circumference of the foot the heart, twice round the foot the height.

Deer, pig, mithun, and buffalo, twice the length of stride the height of the heart from the ground.

Tiger, twice the circumference of *pug* the heart.

## CHAPTER VIII.—Superstitions and Legends.

The creation.

Originally, the face of the earth is stated to have been covered with one vast sea, inhabited by a gigantic worm. The Creator passed over this worm one day, and dropped a small piece of earth, saying "Of this I mean to make a land and people it." The worm replied—"What! you think to make a habitable land of a small piece like this: why, it's absurd: look here, I can swallow it!" Saying this, he swallowed the lump. To his astonishment, it immediately passed out of his body, and increased in size until it became the world we now see. Subsequently, men sprang out of the earth by the will of the gods.

Earthquakes.

The earth is popularly believed to be encircled by a huge serpent, whose head and tail nearly meet. For the greater portion of the year the reptile remains dormant, but occasionally wakes up suddenly, and sees close to him the tail of, what he takes to be, another serpent. He immediately springs at it, and so causes earthquakes.

Snakes.

Some classes of "Kukis" will never kill a snake. They declare snakes to be the writing of the gods, any harm done to them being visited on the inflictor by the gods.

# OUTLINE GRAMMAR.

*o*, unmarked, as the "o" in "p*o*t," "st*o*p," *viz.*, "omâk" "not," "nothing."
*ô* long, as in "b*o*ne" in "shôshôn," " there."
*u* as the "u" in "b*u*ll," "p*u*ll," not as in "h*u*ll" " sk*u*ll."
*û* for the long sound of "oo" in English, *viz.*, "toï-mûn," "a chain."
*ü* having the sound of the French "u" in "l*u*ne," very rare.
*au* having the sound of "ow" in " how," *viz.*, "daumâ," "wife."
*ai* having the sound of "ai" in "aisle," *viz.*, " haishâ," "Râjâ."
*oi*, with the sound of "oi" in "boil," *viz.*, "âjoitâ," "finished."

## (2) Consonants.

All consonants not treated below retain their English pronunciations:—

*c* is discarded, except in the combination "ch;" when hard, "k" is used; when soft "s."
*d* more dental than in English.
*g* always hard, as in "gun."
*h*, carrying the same sound as in English.
*j* as in "joy."
*l*, as in English.
*n* same as in English.
*ñ* with a strong nasal sound.
*ng*, a combination common at the end of a word, pronounced as the "ng" in "singing."
*g* substituted for the deep guttural *k*.
*s* always as in "this," never as in "these."
*sh* as in shall.

Some few combinations of letters have purposely been omitted; partly because the sounds they would convey are so exceedingly rare that practically they are not in use, and partly because the only combinations available would fail to give a sufficiently near approach to the correct pronunciation to render them of value to the student.

It should be borne in mind that every letter, when not accented, is to be pronounced as fully as possible.

# AN OUTLINE GRAMMAR

OF THE

# RANGKHOL-KUKI-LUSHAI LANGUAGE.

THE following sketch of the Kuki language is comprised under three heads:—

(1) Orthography.
(2) Etymology.
(3) Syntax.

## PART I.—ORTHOGRAPHY.

There are sounds in Kuki difficult to reproduce exactly by any combination of letters; these can only be learnt from personal conversation with the people.

The writer has adopted in part the alphabet drawn up as a model by Mr. C. J. Lyall, C.S.

This alphabet, expressing, as it does, the modification of sounds in both vowels and consonants, should be carefully studied. The symbols are not too numerous, and can readly be mastered.

### (1) VOWELS.

*a*, when not marked, always short as in "comp*a*ny," never sharp as in "p*a*n," *viz.*, the "ga" in "gapâ," "my father."

*â* long as in "ah," "f*a*ther," not as in "b*a*ll," *viz.*, "gapâ" "my father."

*à* as in "p*a*n."

*å* the sound of "å" in "b*a*ll."

*e* unmarked as in "th*e*m" "m*e*t" "b*e*d," *viz.*, "enjong," "habit."

*ê* as in "th*ey*" or the "*ai*" in "*ai*m," *viz.*, "jêrbêl," "plates."

*i*, unmarked, as the "i" in "in."

*î* "i" in "machine," *viz.*, "gakî," "my elbow," or "kî," "elbow."

*Abbreviations.*

| | | | |
|---|---|---|---|
| Chap. | .... | .... | Chapter. |
| Lit. | .... | .... | Literally. |
| Adj. | .... | .... | Adjective. |
| B. | .... | .... | Bengali. |
| E. | .... | .... | English. |
| R. K. | .... | .... | Rangkhol-Kuki. |
| J. K. | .... | .... | Jansen-Kuki. |
| L. | .... | .... | Lushai. |

## PREFACE TO OUTLINE GRAMMAR.

In writing this Grammar the compiler has endeavoured as much as possible to avoid the use of arbitrary symbols and accented letters. It is, of course, in many cases absolutely necessary to inform the reader in what manner certain English letters carrying various sounds in different words are to be pronounced in sentences; and in such cases accents have been used. It is difficult in any language to catch the exact pronunciation in any way but from hearing the words spoken, and all that can be arrived at is to convey an approximately correct pronunciation.

A few sounds may have to be omitted by a compiler, owing to the absence of certain symbols; but it is open to question whether the use of these, carrying the exact sound to the author, would be readily grasped by the student.

The compiler has made a brief comparison of the various nialects of the tribes comprised under the head of "Kuki" dap the language known as Lushai in Cachar and on the Assam frontier generally. The grammar itself treats principally of Rangkhol (Kuki), the dialect of that tribe being one the writer is well acquainted with, and being, moreover, one, in his opinion, fairly representative of the grammatical formation of the whole group,—Lushai Poey, Jansens, Tadoïs, &c. The words themselves, of course, differ to a great extent, but the syntactical relations are much the same in all.

The compiler has called this work a "Rangkhol-Kuki-Lushai Grammar." It would not be corre ct to style it a Kuki Grammar, the dialects varying too much, and "Rangkhol" alone would not be understood to refer to "Kukis" at all by the general run of readers. Again, the tribe is so clearly connected with the Lushais that we must include the latter in naming.

*The 29th December 1885.* C. A. SOPPITT.

### (3) Accents—General Rules.

(*a*) In pronouncing unaccented words of two or more syllables, more stress should be laid on the first than on any of the others, "*hon*gro,"* "come."

*Exception.*—In certain compound words the stress is placed on the last syllable, thus, "hong-*noro*," "come again," or "come back."

The sense of the sentence in many cases influences the accentuation. In the above the stress is put on the "noro," to impress on the hearer the fact that he must come back.

(*b*) In sentences and words where the accent rests unequally on two syllables at the expense of the rest, the principal stress is shown thus ("); the lesser thus (′) "hong′nong-rângmôh",=will come back or not."

(*c*) In cases where the same letter is repeated, as at the conclusion and commencement of two syllables in a word, a hyphen is inserted; by being omitted, one of the letters might be left out in the pronunciation, thus; "en-nongro," "open."

(*d*) The symbol (˘) over a letter denotes that it is to be pronounced as shortly as possible.

(*e*) Nouns in declension take the accent on the last syllable as a rule, *viz.*, "vôklê′," "by a pig (inst)."

*Exception.*—In the ablative case the main accent often rests on the centre syllable, thus "râm′kôl"âtâ," "from the jungle."

(*f*) The interrogative sign "môh"† nearly always takes the accent.

## PART II.—ACCIDENCE.

We may divide the Kuki language into eight classes of words, or parts of speech, namely:—

(1) Noun, (2) Adjective, (3) Pronoun, (4) Verb, (5) Adverb, (6) Preposition, (7) Conjunction, (8) Interjection.

The Article, it will be seen, is missing. It is represented by "enkât," or "kât," literally "one," thus "a table" is expressed by "one table."

### 1.—NOUNS.

The nouns are divided into three kinds—(1) common, (2) proper, (3) abstract, and possess gender, number, person, and case.

---

* This is also pronounced "hôngrô."

† See Interrogative "môh," page 52.

### Gender.

The gender of nouns is distinguished in the following ways—

Firstly (*a*)—The feminine from the masculine by different words, as—

| | |
|---|---|
| (1) rûtârtê, a boy. | daumâtê, girl. |
| (2) bâsâl, male (ref. human beings). | nûpâng, female (ref. human beings). |
| (3) mîrim, man | nûreng, woman. |

Secondly (*b*)—By difference of terminations—

| | |
|---|---|
| (1) ârkông, cock | ârnûpâng, hen, *also* "ânnûpang." |
| (2) vâr'pâ, old man | vârnû, old woman. |
| (3) âpâ, father | ânû, mother. |
| (4) âjâl, male (animal) | ânûpâng, female (animals). |

Thirdly (*c*)—By affixing another word—

| | |
|---|---|
| vôk-âjâl, pig (boar) | vôk-ânûpâng, sow (pig, female). |
| sêrhât-âjâl, bull | sêrhât-ânûpâng, cow. |

Qualifying words indicating gender invariably follow the word they qualify, thus, "vôk-âjâl," "boar," and not "âjâl-vôk."

"Nûpâng" may be considered the sign of the feminine when used in connection with human beings, "ânûpâng" is used in reference to animals.

### Number.

There are two numbers only, the singular and the plural. The singular, as in Kachari and Nága, is indicated by the name of the object thus "woman," but sometimes the affix "one," "kât," is used to express the number more clearly,

(1) The plural is formed in all cases by addition of "hai" to the singular, thus :—

| *Singular.* | *Plural.* |
|---|---|
| Mirim, a man | Mirim hai, men. |
| Naitê, child | Naitê hai, children. |
| Rômai, pumpkin | Rômai hai, pumpkins. |
| Vôk, pig | Vôk hai, pigs. |
| Âpâ, father | Âpâ hai, fathers. |
| Sêrhât, cow | Sêrhât hai, cows. |
| Rûtârtê, boy. | Rûtârtê hai, boys. |
| Ting, tree | Ting hai, trees. |
| Râl, war | Râl hai, wars. |
| Rângkhôl, a Rângkhôl | Rângkhôl hai, Rângkhôls. |

(2) In compounds, as a rule, the last word takes the plural termination.

It is not uncommon for the noun to be used in a singular form with a plural sense, thus "man" is substituted for "men," &c.

### Person.

There are three persons, first, second, and third.

### Case.

The Kuki noun is taken as having eight cases.

The case-endings are as follows:—

| *Singular.* | *Plural.* |
|---|---|
| *Nom*. Vôk, pig | Vôk hai, pigs. |
| *Obj*. Vôk, a pig. | |
| *Int.* Vôklê, by or with a pig. | The remaining case endings in the plural are the same as in the singular, the "hai" being inserted. |
| *Dat.* Vôkkâ, to a pig. | |
| *Abl.* Vôk (kôl) âtâ, from a pig. | |
| *Poss.* Vôkanî, of a pig. | |
| *Loc.* Vôkâh, in a pig. | |
| *Voc.* Êkâ vôk, a pig. | |

It will be seen that the nominative and objective have no case endings.

The noun in Kuki is not susceptible of a verbal termination, as is sometimes the case in Kácha Nága; thus, we cannot say "mîrimtâ," "is a man," for "mîrim âhômta;" that is to say, we cannot drop the root of the verb "âhôm," and add the tense terminations direct to the noun.

## 2.—ADJECTIVES.

(*a*) The adjective in Kuki invariably follows the noun it qualifies, thus—

"A good man," "mîrim âsâ," lit., "a man good."

(*b*) There is no change in terminations in adjectives when used in connection with nouns of different gender,—

"A good man," "mîrim âsâ," lit., "man good."

"A good woman," "nûreng âsâ," "woman good."

(*c*) The adjective in Kuki (as in Nága and Kachari) is susceptible of verbal terminations when used with the verb "to be;" thus "will be good" is expressed by the adjective "good," "âsâ," and the future termination of the verb, "âsâ-râng," lit., "will good," the verbal root being omitted.

Again, "it is good," appears as "âsâ," good, "vâ," perfect tense termination, *i.e.*, "âsâtâ," lit., "gooded."

In Nága and Kachari the root of the adjective only is retained when used as a verbal substantive; in Kuki the adjective appears in the full form.

The adjective may be used with the full verb, *i.e.*, without omitting the verbal root; but this form is not quite correct.

"Âsâ," good, "âhôngtâ," it is, should always appear as "âsâtâ," "gooded."

(*d*) Adjectives, as in Nága and Kachari, have a negative form. This negative is formed by affixing "mâk" to the word: thus "âsârâng," "will (be) good;" "âsârângmâk" "will not (be) good."

COMPARISON.

The comparative of adjectives is formed by the addition of "ôl" to the positive, thus—

| | |
|---|---|
| Âsâ, good | Âsâôl, better. |
| Âlîn, big | Âlînôl, bigger. |
| Âjîn, small. | Âjînôl, smaller. |

The superlative degree is formed by changing the "ôl" into "tâk;" thus —

| | | |
|---|---|---|
| âsâ, good | âsâôl, better | âsâtâk, best. |
| âlîn, big | âlînôl, bigger | âlîntâk, biggest. |
| âjîn, small | âjînôl, smaller | âjîntâk, smallest. |

*Exception.*—One or two adjectives have an irregular superlative degree; thus, "shâmâk," "bad," comparative "sâhâôlmâk," superlative "sâloïtâk," the "tâk" is preceded by "loï," and the "mâk" omitted. "Shâmâk," it will be seen, is merely the negative form of âsâ," "good," the first "â" being omitted and an "h" added. The comparative sign is inserted before the negative termination "mâk."

(*a*) NUMERAL ADJECTIVES.

The following are the numerals up to ten:—

| | |
|---|---|
| One, enkât (kât). | Six, gărûk. |
| Two, en-nî. | Seven, sârî. |
| Three, entûm. | Eight, gărît. |
| Four, mîlî. | Nine, gûôk. |
| Five, ringâh. | Ten, shôm. |

(1) There are no single words to express numbers between ten and nineteen, but ten-one, ten-two, &c., appear. Twenty

is expressed by "ten-two," "shôm-nî" (twice ten). Thirty, forty, by ten-by-three, ten by-four, &c.

"One hundred" is "rajâ-kât," "two hundred," "rajâ-nî," and so on.

"One thousand" is "shângkât;" "two thousand," "shâng-nî," &c.

(2) In expressing numerals having reference to money of to animals certain prefixes are used, thus:—

"Twenty rupees" (dâr) "shômnî" (rupees ten-by-two).

"Thirty-five (rupees)" "dârshômtûm-lê ringăh."

"Dâr" is a sign that the amount refers to money, but "dâr" has no meaning of itself, when not affixed to numerals.

The "ringâh," "five," it will be seen, is preceded by "lê." This word has no separate meaning, but is used to denote where the broken numbers commenced; thus, in the sentence "dârshômtûm lê ringâh" we have rupees ten-by-thirty-and-five, the place of "and" being taken by "lê."

(3) In speaking of houses, the numeral is preceded by the prefix "dông;" thus, "forty houses" does not appear as "în shôm mîlî," *i.e.*, în (houses) shôm mîlî (forty), but as "dông-shôm mîlî."

(4) In all cases the nouns designating the numerals are placed first, the numbers following.

(5) There is no prefix used in reference to human beings.

## 3.--PRONOUNS.

Pronouns in Kuki are divided into four classes—

(1) Personal, (2) Relative and Interrogative, (3) Demonstrative, (4) Adjective.

(*a*) (1) PERSONAL.

| | |
|---|---|
| (1) gê, I. | (1) gênî, we. |
| (2) nâng, you | (2) nângnî, you. |
| (3) {mî / âmâ} he, she, it. | (3) {mîhai / âmâhai} they. |

(*b*) For the first person there are two forms in use besides "gê;" thus "gênî" (the real plural "we") is commonly used with the meaning of "I;" "gêmâ" is also used.

The plural "gênî" is nearly alway substituted for "gêhai" or "gênîhai," which are the true plurals ("we"), though the forms are rarely sued.

(*c*) The pronouns are declined in the same way as nouns. Their possessive case-ending can only be used with the first and second persons singular; thus, "gêmâ," "mine;" "nângmâ," "yours." We cannot say "mimâ," meaning "his," or "gênîmâ," meaning "ours."

(*d*) In other words, where possession is shown, the personal pronoun appears in the first or second person singular, irrespective of whether the sense be singular or plural.

(*e*) It will be seen that a great deal of liberty is allowed in the use of the personal pronoun in its singular and plural forms.

Thus, we see the plural "gênî," "we," the possessive "gêmâ," "mine," and "gê," all used to represent the first person singular.

In the plural the termination "hai" (the plural sign) is used in the third person, "mî hai," but not in the second, or the first.

### Relative and Relative Interrogative.

These pronouns are—

(1) tûmôh, who?
(2) îmôh, which?
(3) îmôh, what?—"îtòmoh" sometimes used, meaning more, "what's the matter?"

These are declined like substantives, there being no possessive case-ending.

The plural of "who," "tûmôh," is formed by adding the regular plural sign "hai," "tûhaimôh."

This sign "hai" is placed next to the root "tû" and before the "môh."

### Demonstrative Pronouns.

These are—

| | |
|---|---|
| (1) âmâhai, this | (1) âmâ or shôhai, kûhai, that. |
| (2) âmâhaihi, these | (2) kûhaikû, those. |

(*a*) The plural is formed by inserting the plural sign in the middle of the word "âmâ-hai-hi."

(*b*) "Kûhi" is very rarely used for "that;" kûhaikû being made to do duty for singular and plural.

(*c*) Sometimes, but very rarely, "mi," "it, she, he" is put in the place of "kûhi," "that."

### ADJECTIVE PRONOUNS.

These are—

(1) Other .................. âdâng-râmdâng.
(2) Another .............. mîdâng.*
(3) Everyone ........... enkât-kât.
(4) The same ............ mûnkât.
(5) So many ............... îdor.
(6) How many .......... îdôrmôh.
(7) Such ..................... shohai, îhai.

## 4.—VERBS.

On a former page it has been shown that adjectives are susceptible of verbal terminations, and in many cases, when used with "to be," take the place of the verb in a sentence; thus, "it is a good jhúm," "loi âsâtâ," or "mi loi âsâtâ." In this sentence the verb "is" does not appear, the tense termination "tâ" being affixed to the adjective, "âsâ" "good."

Owing to the verb in Kuki being interchangeable and in some cases compoundable with adjectives, other verbs and even separate affixes, the sense and force is often greatly enhanced. Numerous examples will be given in order that the variations of the verb in this respect may be clearly demonstrated.

The root of the verb, it will be seen, remains perfectly regular throughout the conjugation.

As in Kachári, the verb is found in its simplest form in the Imperative, that mood not taking a separate termination as in Kacha Nága.

In common with Kachári and Nága, the temporal affix remains unchanged for all persons in both numbers; thus, "râng," the future termination, is the same for I, thou, he, we, you, and they, the nominative case termination in the sentence demonstrating the number and person of the verb. There is no irregular verb in Kuki in the sense of a verb whose tense terminations vary, but the great difficulty lies in assigning the proper force to verbs compounded with other roots and affixes.

The following is the conjugation of the verb "hômrôshê," "to be."

---

* "Another," "midâng," is generally used in the sense of "another person" or "man." In speaking of animals and inanimate objects "âdâng" or "râmdâng" takes the place of "mîdâng;" "enkât-kât," "every one," also means "each one."

### "*Âhômrôshê*," *to be.*

### INDICATIVE MOOD.

#### 1—PRESENT TENSE.

| *Singular.* | *Plural.* |
|---|---|
| Gê âhôm, I am | Gêni âhôm, we are. |
| Nâng âhôm, thou art | Nângni âhôm, you are. |
| Mi âhôm, he is | Mihai âhôm, they are |

#### 2—PAST.

| *Singular.* | *Plural.* |
|---|---|
| Gê âhômtâ, I was, &c. | Gêni âhômtâ, we, &c. |

#### 3—FUTURE.

| *Singular.* | *Plural.* |
|---|---|
| Gê âhômrâng, *or* hômrâng, I shall be, &c. | Gêni hômrâng *or* hômrâng, we, &c. |

#### 4—PRESENT PERFECT.

| *Singular.* | *Plural.* |
|---|---|
| Gê tinâ âhômtâ, I have, &c. | Gêni tinâ âhômtâ, we, &c. |

PROGRESSIVE.—Tinâ âkhin kin hom, have been, &c.

#### 5—PAST PERFECT.

| *Singular.* | *Plural.* |
|---|---|
| Gê âhôm jôïtâ (joitâ), I had, &c. | Gêni âhôm jôïtâ, we, &c. |

#### 6—FUTURE PERFECT.

| *Singular.* | *Plural.* |
|---|---|
| Gê âhôm jôïrâng, I shall have, &c. | Gêni âhôm jôïrâng, we, &c. |

### IMPERATIVE MOOD.

| *Singular.* | *Plural.* |
|---|---|
| Âhômrô (hômrô), be | Âhômrôï, be you. |

### POTENTIAL MOOD.

#### PRESENT TENSE.

| *Singular.* | *Plural.* |
|---|---|
| (1) Gê âhôm tê, I may or can be | Gênî âhôm tê, we, &c. |

#### PAST.

| *Singular.* | *Plural.* |
|---|---|
| (2) Gê âhômtêtâ, I might, would be. | Gêni âhômtêtâ, we, &c. |

#### PRESENT PERFECT.

| *Singular.* | *Plural.* |
|---|---|
| (3) Gê âhômtêtâ, I, &c. | Gêni âhômtêtâ, we, &c. |

## SUBJUNCTIVE MOOD.

### Present Tense.

| | *Singular.* | *Plural.* |
|---|---|---|
| (1) | Gê âhômentê, if I am | Gêni âhômentê, if we, &c. |

### Past Tense.

| | *Singular.* | *Plural.* |
|---|---|---|
| (2) | Gê âhômentê, if I was | Gêni âhômentê, if we, &c. |

Not used in other tenses.

## INFINITIVE MOOD.

*Present.*—Ahômrô shê, to be, or hôm rôshê.

## PARTICIPLES.

*Present.*—Âhômlê, being. *Perfect.*—Âhômêntê (*or* âhômenjû), having been.

### *Remarks. –Indicative Mood.*

(*a*) It has been mentioned that the verb appears in its simplest forms in the Imperative (singular), but it will be seen that in the Present Tense the root is still more curtailed. This "âhom" in the tense in question is, perhaps, more of a colloquial form than anything else, as the sense would be as correctly conveyed by "âhômro," thus, "gê âhômrô" I am.

(*b*) The Future is given as "âhômrâng," or "hômrâng." It is here necessary to point out when the "â" should be retained and when omitted.

(1) In the Indicative Present, when the form "âhôm" is used, the "â" must always appear; should "âhomrô" be used, the "â" may be omitted: thus, "gê hômrô," I am.

*Exception.*—When the interrogative "môh" is affixed, the "â" must be retained; thus, "nâng âhôm," *or* "âhômrômôh," "you are," and not "nâng âhôm (rô) môh."

(2) In answering a query the "â" is sometimes omitted, thus, "nâng âhômrângmôh?" "will you be?" "gêhômrâng" "I will be." Here "hômrâng" conveys a more complete sense, the sentence meaning "I (certainly) will be," "(without doubt) will be." In such cases it will be seen the verb gains considerably in force by the omission of the "â."

(3) In other cases the "â" is dropped for the sake of euphony: thus, in the Infinitive "âhômrôshê" often appears as "hômrôshê," the sense conveyed being exactly the same in either case.

(c)(1) The Present Perfect is formed by placing "tînâ" before the verb; thus, "gê tînâ âhômtâ," "I have been," "tînâ" means literally "before" or "formerly;" thus, "gê (I) tînâ (before or formerly) âhômtâ (was)"="I formerly was" or "I have been."

(2) The progressive form "tînâ âkhin-kin hôm(âhômtâ)," "have been," is rarely used: "âkhin-kin" points to a progressive action.

(d) *Past Perfect.*—This tense is formed in a peculiar way. The "âhôm," "be," is followed by "joïtâ," literally meaning "finished," "completed." The "joï," it will be seen, takes the past termination; thus, "gê âhôm joïtâ," "I finished *or* completed to be," *i.e.*, "I had been."

(e) *The Future Perfect.*—This tense is formed in the same way as the Past Perfect: "gê âhôm joïrâng," "I shall completed to be," *i.e.*, "I shall have been."

"Joï," it will be seen, takes the future termination, "âhôm" remaining unchanged.

*Imperative Mood.*

(a) In this mood a plural termination is formed by adding "ï" to the singular, "âhômrôï" *or* "hômrôï," "be you."

The plural form is not in common use.

*Potential Mood.*

(a) This mood is only used in the present and past tenses, "âhômtê," âhômtêtâ."

The sign of the mood "te" is placed between the verbal root and the tense termination in the past.

*Subjunctive Mood.*

(a) In this mood the tense termination "entê" does not vary. The "entê" also appears in the perfect participle, "âhômentê," "having been."

*Agent.*

The agent or person doing is expressed by affixing "pû" and sometimes "pa."

Thus, "âhômpû," "the stayer, the one staying."

"Âhômrângpû," "the one of will stay."

"Âhômpûhai," *plural*, "the ones who stay or staying."

"Âhômrângpûhai," *plural*, "the ones who will stay, &c."

"Pâ" may be substituted for "pû" in any of the above, without changing the sense.

### *Force given to Verbs.*

In order to give extra force to the verb, the word "gănêt" is frequently placed between the root and the tense termination. This "gănêt" has no meaning of its own, but, when used with the verb, conveys a sense of completeness, and puts the question beyond doubt.

Thus, "gê âhômrâng," "I will be or remain."

"Gê âhôm-gănêt-râng," "I will (without the least doubt, for certain, remain)."

"Nâng ahômrâng," "you will remain."

"Nâng âhômgănêt-râng," "you (must; it is settled) will remain."

"Nâng ârôt-tâ," "you ran away."

"Nâng ârôt-gănêt-tâ," "(it is beyond doubt: beyond question) you ran away."

"Mi âhôngrângmôh," "will he come."

"Mi âhôngrâng, *or* hôngrâng," "he will come."

"Mi âhông-gănêt-râng," "(it is certain) he will come."

The participles are largely used in Kuki, as is the case in Kachári and Kacha Nága.

They are very often combined with the agent expressed by "pû" *or* "pâ" already alluded to.

Thus—(1) "The man I saw yesterday,"
"gê mijânâ âmûpû," *literally*, "the one (man) yesterday seen (by) me."
"âmûpûkâ" is sometimes used in the place of "âmûpû."

(2) "The deer when it saw the man ran away."
"Sâjûk mirim âmûênjû ârôt-tâ," *literally*, "the deer, seeing, or having seen, the man, ran away."

(3) "The dâk-runners have arrived."
"dâkjôngpû âtûngtâ," *literally*, "the dâk ones have arrived."

### *Passive Voice.*

The passive voice, as in Kachari and Nága, is formed by prefixing the past participle of the verb to the different tenses of (â) "niroshê," "to be," "become."

The conjugation of (â) "niroshê," "to become," is quite regular.

Âgôiênjû ânitâ }
Âgôiênjû âni } "I am called: being called, &c."

"Âgôiênjû ânitâ" "I was called, &c."

## NEGATIVE VERBS.

The negative force is given to the verb not by prefixing a word or syllable, but by affixing "mâk," "nimâk," to the verb.

The conjugation of the verb "hòmrô," "to be," in its negative form is given below:—

### (1) PRESENT TENSE.

| *Singular.* | | *Plural.* |
|---|---|---|
| Gê âhôm nôni, | I am not, be not | Gêni âhmôu ôni, we, &c. |

### (2) PAST.

| *Singular.* | | *Plural.* |
|---|---|---|
| Gê âhômtâ nôni, | I was not, &c. | Gêni âhômtâ nôni, we, &c. |

### (3) FUTURE.

Gê âhômâng (ni) mâk
*also*
Âhômtê râng nimâk
} I will not, &c.

### (4) PRESENT PERFECT.

| *Singular.* | | *Plural.* |
|---|---|---|
| Gê tinâ âhômmâk, | I have not | Gêni tinâ âhômmâk, we, &c. |

### (5) PAST PERFECT.

| *Singular.* | | *Plural.* |
|---|---|---|
| Gê âhôm jôïmâüng, | I had not, &c. | Gêni âhôm jôïmâüng, we had not, &c- |

### (6) FUTURE PERFECT.

| *Singular.* | | *Plural.* |
|---|---|---|
| Gê âhôm jôïnôni, | I shall not have, &c. | Gêni âhôm jôïnôni, we, &c. |

## IMPERATIVE MOOD.

| *Singular.* | *Plural.* |
|---|---|
| Âhôm-nôrô, be not. | Âhôm norôï, be not (you). |

## POTENTIAL MOOD.

### (1) PRESENT TENSE.

| *Singular.* | | *Plural.* |
|---|---|---|
| Gê âhômtê nôni, | I may not, *or* can't | Gê âhôm tê nôni, we, &c. |

(2) Past.

| *Singular.* | *Plural.* |
| --- | --- |
| Gê âhômtê tânêni, I might, *or* could not, &c. | Gêni âhômtê tânôni, we, &c. |

SUBJUNCTIVE MOOD.

(1) Present.

| *Singular.* | | *Plural.* |
| --- | --- | --- |
| Gê âhôm nôentê | if I am not | Gêni âhôm nôentê, we, &c. |

(2) Past and other tenses not used.

PARTICIPLES.

*Present.* Âhôm (mâk) lê (very rare), not being.
*Perfect.* Âhôm nôenjû, not been, having not been, &c.

INFINITIVE.

*Present.* Âhôm nôrôshê,. not to be.

*Remarks.*

(*a*) "Mâk" and "mimâk" are the true negatives, though as seen in the verb above, a considerable variation in the negative sign takes place, "nô," "nôni" being substituted for "mâk,"

(*b*) In the Present Tense we see "nòni" and not "mâk" as the negative sign; "gê âhômmâk" could be understood, though not grammatically correct. It is probable, however, that it would be confounded with "gêômâk," meaning "not I," *i.e.*, some one else.

(*c*) In the same manner in the Past Tense it would not do to substitute "mâk" for "nôni," as in the former case "gê âhômtâmâk" might convey the sense "it was not I," and not "I was not."

(*d*) In the future two forms are in use (1) "ni mâk," and (2) âhôm têrâng nimâk."

The latter, though used for "I will not," conveys the sense of "will not (be able)," and should in reality belong to the Potential Mood.

(*e*) In the Present Perfect "mâk" appears as the negative sign, and "nôni" does not appear.

(*f*) The Past Perfect is formed in a peculiar way: "gê âhôm jôïtâ," "I had been," does not appear as "gê âhôm jôïtâmâk," which would be the regular negative form, but as "gê âhôm jôïmâüng," "I had not been." The past termination "tâ" is dropped and the "k" in "mâk," while "üng" is added. Both are dropped for the sake of euphony; thus, "âhômjôïtâmâküng."

The full form would be hard to pronounce as one word, and would sound anything but well.

(*g*) In the Future Perfect, the future sign "râng" is dropped, and "nôni" affixed. The context in both this case and the former is supposed to show in what tense the verb is.

*Remarks on Imperative.*

The singular (negative) is formed by prefixing "no" to the "ro;" thus, "âhôngrô," "âhôm (nô) rô." The plural in the same manner is formed by prefixing "nô" to "rôï;" thus, "âhômrôï" be (you), "âhôm (nô) rôï" be not ("you.")

*Potential Mood.*

(*a*) The tenses of this mood, in the negative verb, are formed by affixing "nônî."

*Subjunctive Mood.*

(*a*) In this mood the negative sign is affixed to the root of the verb, and between it and its tense termination "nônî" appears as "nô."

*Participles.*

(*a*) The form "âhômmâklê" is rare, âhômnôênjû being in common use for both Present and Perfect.

*Infinitive Mood.*

As in the Imperative, the "rô" is preceded by "nô," the sign of the Infinitive "shây" following.

There is so great a license allowed in the use of the negative signs that it is difficult in all cases to lay down hard-and-fast rules, but the above examples will have shown the sign as generally used.

CAUSATIVE VERBS.

(*a*) These are formed by the root of the verb (the principal verb) followed by "pêgrô" (pêrô) "to give" in its various tenses; thus, "en-pêrô," "show," "en-pêroshê," "to show," "to give to see," "en-pêrâng," *or* "pêrâng," "will show, will give to see."

(*b*) *Relation of cause and effect.*—The relation of cause and effect is expressed by the word "kânjû," thus,—

" Mîsâ ârhât kânjû âhômmâk."
" On account of the sun's heat did not come."

" Rû arhât kânjû shâmâk."
" On account of the heavy rain is bad."

" Ânâ kânjû âhômnônî."
" By reason of, or on account of, sickness cannot come."

## COMPOUND VERBS.

(*a*) As already mentioned, verbs are compoundable with other verbs, and even separate affixes, the sense and force being greatly enhanced.

The following examples will illustrate the various changes undergone by the verb in these cases:—

(*b*) The sense of repetition is conveyed, not by affixing another word, but by inserting "nôg" between the root of the verb and the tense termination, in all moods, except the Imperative and Infinitive. In these latter "nôgrô," the full form, sometimes appears:—

(1) "Gê âhông (nôg) râng," "I will return," *lit.*, "I will (again) come."

(2) "Nâng âhông (nôg) tâ," "you have returned" *or* "you returned," *lit.*, "you have (again) come."

(3) "Gêni tô (nôg) râng," "we will re-do," *lit.*, "we will again do."

(4) "Nâng tô (nôg) tâ," "you have re-done," *lit.*, "you have done again" *or* "again done."

In the Imperative and Infinitive Moods—

(1) Âhông-nôgro, *or* âhôngrô-nôgrô, "come again."

As a rule, the first "rô" is dropped, and it would be perhaps as well not to consider the Imperative and Infinitive as exceptions; but to look upon them as following the other moods, and inserting "nôg" between the root and tense termination: thus, in the Infinitive "âhôngnôgrôshê," "to again come," "to come again," and not "âhôngro-nôgrôshê," "to come again."

(*c*) A sense of haste is conveyed by the insertion of "rât" between the verbal root and tense termination, thus—

| | | |
|---|---|---|
| (1) | "Mi âhôngtâ" | "he is come: has come." |
| (2) | "Mi âhong (rât) tâ." | "he is quickly come: come quick; *or* come in haste." |
| (3) | "Nâng âhông (rât) rô." | "come you quick: in haste, at once come." |
| (4) | "Gêni âhông (rât) tâ." | "we have come at once." |
| (5) | "Nâng âhông (rât) nôrô," | "you come not quickly," *or* "do not come quick." |
| (6) | "Gê âhông (rât) mâk." | "I have not come in haste, *or* quickly." |

(*d*) By using the negative signs "mâk" and "nô" *or* "nôrô," the sense of "not quick," *i.e.*, "slowly," is conveyed, but the more correct way of stating this is by replacing "rât" by "jâm," thus—

(1) "Gê âhông (jâm) tâ" "I have come slowly," *i.e.*, "not fast."

(2) "Nâng âhông (jâm) râng môh?" "will you come slowly?" *i.e.*, not fast, "môh"=sign of interrogative."

(3) "Gêni âhông-jâmrâng" "we have come slowly.'

(*e*) A very great emphasis is given to the verb by the use of the word "vâki" inserted between the root and termination, thus—

(1) "Âhông (vâkï) rô" "come (right) here," "come close here," "exactly here," &c.

(2) "Gê âhông (vâkï) rând" "I will come exactly there or here."

(3) "Nâng âhông (vâkï) tâ" "you have come right here or there," *or* "exactly here or there."

(*f*) The sense of "very," "very much," "exceedingly," &c., is given to the verb by "bâk," thus,—

(1) "Ânâtâ" "is ill" ("anâ," ill, "tâ," verbal termination with root suppressed).

"Ônâ (bâk) tâ," "is very *or* exceedingly ill."

(2) "Âl-lâhtâ," "is far."

"Âl-lâh (bâk) tâ," "is very far."

(3) "Ânâï tâ," "is near."

"Ânâï (bâk) tâ," "is very near," "quite close."

In the above examples "ill," "far," and "near" are compounded with the verb, and then again compounded with the word "bâk."

(*g*) In certain cases "nê-ôk" is used to express the superlative "very" or "exceedingly," "very much," &c., thus—

(1) "Gê nêôktâ" "is very sweet (to eat)," "exceedingly sweet."

(2) "Mi gênêôktâ" "it (the fruit or vegetable) is very sweet," "exceedingly sweet."

(*h*) The sense of completion is given to the verb by inserting "vâr":—

(1) "Kam âjôï (vâr) tâmôh," "is the work entirely (quite) finished."

(2) "Mîrim âhông (vâr) tâmôh," "have the men (all) come."

(3) "Âhông (vâr tâ") " (all) have come," "everyone have come," *i.e.*, none remain to come.

(*i*) The sense of "must" is given to the verb in the following way:—

(1) "Gê âhông râng," "I will come."
"Gê hongrâng-gênî," "I will come certainly," "I must come," "it is settled I will come," &c.

## 5.—ADVERBS.

The Adverbs are of the following kinds—

(1) Manner.
(2) Time.
(3) Place.

### (*a*) Adverbs of Manner.

These are—

| | |
|---|---|
| How | îtinmoh. |
| Quickly | enrângro. |
| Ably: well | âsâ (âsâtâ). |
| Thus (in this way) | nêâng hîn. |
| In that way | hâmâhâ (nâmâhângshôn). |
| Many | âtâm. |
| Few | âtomtê. |
| Slowly | toï ajâm. |
| Alone | enkâtvai. |
| Badly | shâmâk jêah. |

Adverbs in Kuki do not, as a rule, take tense terminations directly attached to their own root, the verbal root being omitted, in the way they do in Kachcha Nága, thus, it is not correct to say "hêanghin*tâ*" for "hêanghin âhomta," "it is in this way," "like this."

### (*b*) Adverbs of Time.

| | |
|---|---|
| To-day | âvûn. |
| To-morrow | nângtûk. |
| Yeterday | mîjân. |
| The day after | nângtûkpên. |

| | |
|---|---|
| Now | âtûn. |
| Always | ânîtin-ânîtin. |
| Sometimes | aitîgâmoh: aitîgâmôh.* |
| Before | tinâ. |
| Afterwards | hinûngâ lâganâ. |
| Soon | enrângro. |
| Late | âshôtâ. |
| When | itîgmoh. |
| In the morning | jîngâh. |

(*c*) Adverbs of Place.

| | |
|---|---|
| Here | hîtîngâh. |
| There | shôshôn, *also* shoting. |
| Where | kotîngmôh. |
| Within | âshûng (âh). |
| Behind | enöûng (âh); enûngâh. |
| Above | âsâgâ. |
| Below | âtângâh. |
| Elsewhere | âdângâ. |
| Far | âlhâh. |
| Near | an-nâï. |

Some of these adverbs take verbal terminations directly affixed to the root; thus, "an-nâï," "near;" "an-nâïtâ," "is near."

## 6.—PREPOSITIONS.

The words corresponding to the English prepositions follow the noun as they do in Kachari and in Nága, and never precede it. They are :—

| | |
|---|---|
| Among | ârîlâh âsûng. |
| Around | "ervailtâ," sometimes pronounced "ervêltâ." |
| Behind | ennûng. |
| Between | âlai-âh. |
| Below | ânûïâ. |
| With | jânpûï. |
| Without | âbûîtê (having or being nothing). |
| For | itô, as "for what," îmâto *or* î-ïto. |
| From | âtâ. |
| To | âh. |

* Lit., "at times, at times."

| | |
|---|---|
| In | rîlâ.* |
| Up to | gên shûök.† |
| Like (like this) | îdorhî. |
| On account of, *or* for this reason. | âniâh. |
| After | en-nûng. |

"Against" as in Nága, is denoted generally by the locative case as "tîng (âh) ârnêltâ, he leans (against the tree)."

## 7.—CONJUNCTIONS.

The Conjunction is very rare, the participle taking its place; thus, "I went and returned," "gênî fêtââh" or (gê gâfêâh)‡ "gâhôngnôgtâ," literally "I having gone returned." Because (for that) nêhânghî.

"Until," or "so long as," is expressed in the following manner:—" Kâm nâtômâshing," " work until you do." Here the " nâ " preceding the "tô" is put in apparently merely for the sake of euphony; "mâ" is the negative "tomâ," "not doing," thus literally the sentence should be translated " work while you not doing," equal to "work until you do."

The disjunctives "neither" and "nor" are not expressed: "nâng (â) hôngmâk," "gênî hôngmâk," "you came not," " I came not."

## 8.—INTERJECTIONS.

The more common of these are—

| | | |
|---|---|---|
| Hush! | jòng-nôrò! | *lit.*, " don't speak." |
| Alas! | hai! | |
| Bravo! | âsâjîk! | |
| Hallo! | ôi! | |

# PART III.—SYNTAX.

It is very difficult in a language so little known as Kuki to lay down a complete Syntax; and, though a few rules are given below as a guide, the student will in most cases be able to form a more correct idea of the formation of the language and the variations the parts of speech undergo when brought into syntactical relation with one another, from the illustrative sentences attached.

* "Rilâ" means "inside" in certain cases; also in "the middle," "amidst," "among."

† " Gên shûok," meaning literally "until reached," "until got to."

‡ This "gêgâfêâh" is idiomatic.

## General Rules.

(*a*) The verb does not agree in person and number with its subject; but remains unchanged, the plural or singular significance being conveyed by the subject.

(*b*) The adjective follows a noun.

(*c*) When two verbs come together, the former must be in the Infinitive Mood.

(*d*) As a general rule ideas in Kuki are conveyed in as few words as possible, but an ellipsis is not allowable when the employment of it would occasion obscurity or weaken the force of the sentence.

(*e*) The interrogative is shown, not by an inflection of the voice, but by affixing a word to the sentence. This word "môh," has no separate meaning of its own. This "môh," as a sign of interrogation, should never be omitted, as the sense of a sentence might be completely changed.

"Ásâ," for example, in spite of any inflection, would almost always be taken by a Kuki to mean "it is good," and that the fact of its being was beyond question: "ásâmôh" would show the interrogation.

*Sentences illustrating the use of the Noun or Substantive.*

## I.—NOUNS.

### (*a*) Gender.

| | |
|---|---|
| (The men and women) have come. | (mîrimhai, nûvenghai) âhông-tâ. |
| (The girls and boys) are playing. | (dôngmâ têhai), rûtârtêhai erdailê. |
| (The buffalo) is savage. | (shêloï) âhaitâ. |
| There are (bulls and cows). | (âjâl, sêrhât ânûpâng) âhôm-tâ. |
| (Men and women) are working. | (mîrimhai, nûvenghai) kâm-âtölê. |
| (The old man) has come. | (târpâ) âhôngtâ. |
| (The old woman) has come. | (târnû) âhôngtâ. |
| The married (men and women) do not dance. | (mîrimhai, nûvenghai) daumâ âmânpâ,* rûtârâmân† lâm-mâk. |

* Daumâ âmânpâ, *lit.*, getter of a wife.

† Rûtârâmân, *lit.*, getter of husband.

### (b) NUMBER.

| | |
|---|---|
| (The children) are bathing | (naitêhai) ershîl.* |
| (A man) has come | (mîrim) âhông-tâ. |
| (The men) hav ecome | (mîrimhai) âhongtâ. |
| Where is the (mithan)? | (shîl) kôtîngmôh?† |
| The (mithans) are in the jungle. | (shîlhai) râmâh âhôm.‡ |
| (The villager) is coming | [kûhai (kûmîrim)] âhông-lê. |
| The villagers (have come) | [kûhai (kûmîrimhai)] âhôngtâ. |
| Where is (the woman)? | (nûveng) kôtîngmôh (âhôm)? |
| Where are (the women)? | (nûvenghai) kôtîngmôh (âhôm)? |
| I hear (a tiger) | gê (kâmgêî) gânrît.§ |
| I heard (the tigers) | gê (kâmgêîhai) gânrîttâ. |
| Is (the dog) barking? | (ûî) enrâmôh. |
| (The dogs) are barking | [ûîhai] enrâm [enrâmlê]. |

### (c) CASE.

| | |
|---|---|
| Where does he live (in the village)? | mi (kûah) (kôtîngmôh âhôm) kôînmôh âhôm?‖ |
| Is he coming (from his house)? | (înâtâ, âhong (lî) môh? |
| Cut (with a knife) | (gâtâlrîâlâ) jêmrô. |
| (Give me) a plantain | (gêâh) môt pêrô (pêrô). |
| The deer came (from the jungle) | (râmâtâ) sâjûkhai âhôngtâ. |
| I gave (them) money | gê { (mihaïâh) shûm âpêtâ (âpêgtâ) âmâhaiâh. |
| The men (of that village are) strong | shôhaikûâtâ mîrimhai ernâk âhôm. |

---

* "Ershîl," the verb in this sentence, commonly appears in the past tense.

† In this sentence the verb is understood and expressed, *lit.*, "where mithan.'

‡ "Âhôm,"—*see.**

§ "Gânrît" is peculiarly idiomatic, "anrît" is "to hear," generally, with the "gân" it signifies that the person speaking hears. This "gân" appears before a great number of verbs, and invariably conveys the same sense.

‖ "Kôinmôh," *lit.*, in what house?

| | |
|---|---|
| Take wood (from the fire) | (mêâtâ) tîng lârô. |
| I will shoot (a pigeon) | gê (pêrbâlî) kâprâng. |
| Bring (them) some water | dûî { mîbaiâh / amâhaiâh* } hôngjôîrô. |
| I come (from the plains) | gê (phaiâtâ) âhôngtâ. |
| (His child) is dead | mîmâ âmâ nâitê âtîtâ. |
| The man's head was broken | (mîrim) lû† âlu âkoitâ. |
| There are no fish (in the river) | (dûîkôngâh) gănâ ômâk ‡ |
| It is (his) cow | (âmâ) sêrhât âhôm. |
| It is (my) duty | (gêmâ) kâm âhôm. |
| The owner (of the house) has not come | (sâkor) § âjôngpû âhôngmâk. |
| Give (me) a little | âjîn (gêâh) pêrô (pêrô). |
| Strike (a match) | (mêjî) entôrô. |
| Boil (the water) | (dûî) mêâh âlûmrô. ‖ |
| Give him (a gun) | âmâkâ (sîlai) pêrô. |
| Buy a spear (from the shop-keeper). | (gûlâ-âjôngpûâtâ âtâ ôfê erjarô). |
| There is nothing (in the house) | (înâh) nênûm ômâk |

## ADJECTIVES.

| | |
|---|---|
| A (good) jhúm | loî (âsâ). |
| A (deep) river | dûîkûng (ântûktâ). |
| A (bad) man | mîrim (shâmâk) |
| A (high) hill | lâmtûng (âshê). |
| Is he (strong) | âmââh (ernâk) âhômtâmôh ¶ *or* âmâ (ârhâttâ). |
| The liquor (is good) | jû (âsâtâ). |
| Bring a (long) cane | êtîng (âshê) ** hôngjôîrô. |

## Adjectives (Comparison of).

| | |
|---|---|
| Men are (taller) than women | mîrimhai, nûvênghăi (âshêôl). |
| Boys are (stronger) than girls | naipânghai, dôngmâtêhai (ârhâtôl). |

---

* Also "mîhaishô," "âmâhaishô."

† The sign of the possessive is omitted for the sake of euphony.

‡ The verb is here understood.

§ *See* †.

‖ *Lit.*, make warm.

¶ *Lit.*, has he strength ?

** The verbal term termination is added to the adjective "âsâ" "good."

| | |
|---|---|
| He is (the bigger) of the two | ennîâh âmâ (âlînôl). |
| This house (is larger than that) | ámâhai în, shôhai în (âlinôl). |
| The elephant is (stronger) than the rhinoceros. | shaipûï gêndâ (ârhâtôl) |
| This is (sweeter) than that | âmâhai, shôhai (âtûïôl). |
| These hills are (higher) than those | âmâhaihi lâmtûng,* kûhaiku lâmtûng (âshêôl). |
| This is the (last) of all | âmâhai (âlintâk). |
| Give me (the largest) | gêâh (âlintâk) pêrô. |
| Which is (the biggest)? | imôh (âlintâk).? |
| This is the (largest) house | âmâ în (âlintâk). |

### ADJECTIVES, NUMERAL.

| | |
|---|---|
| Bring (forty coolies) | (mîrim shômmîlî) hôngjôïrô. |
| Only (three men) have come | (mîrim entûm) vai âhôngtâ. |
| I shot (two deer) | gê (sâjûkennî) âkâptâ. |
| Buy (six fowls) | (âr gărûk) erjarô. |

### PRONOUNS.—PERSONAL.

| | |
|---|---|
| (I) shall go | (gê) fêrâng. |
| (We) are coming | (gêni) âhông (âhônglê). |
| (He) is alone | [âmâ (mî)] enkât vai, âhôm. |
| Where are (you) going | (nâng) kôtîngmôh nîfê†? |
| Where are (they) | (âmâhai) kôtîngmôh âhôm?‡ |
| Will (you) come | (nâng) âhông râng môh? |
| Have you seen (my) dog | (gêmâ) ûi âmûtâmôh? |
| Give (me) the gun | shêlai [gêâh, (gêni)] pêrô. |
| Show me (his) house | (âmâ§) în ermûrô. |
| (We) can see | (gêni) enrôtê. |

* The noun very often remains in the singular with a plural significance.

† "Fêlê" would be the regular form of the verb: the "lê" is dropped, as is often the case when the present participle is used. The "nî" is purely idiomatic, and is used apparently for the sake of euphony.

‡ The sign of the interrogative might be attached to the verb, and the "môh" being dropped from the "kôtîng," thus, "kôtîngâhômmôh" would be quite correct.

§ The sign of the possessive is rarely used with "he, she, it."

### Other Pronouns.

| | |
|---|---|
| [The men (who) ran away] have come. | (ârôtpûhai*) âhôngtâ. |
| Where is the man (whom) you saw? | nangkê mûloïpâ kôting môh âhôm?† |
| The cooli s (who) came, returned | mîrim (kûlî) âhômhai fênôgtâ‡ |
| (Who) has come? | (tûmôh) âhôngtâ? |
| (Whose) cow? | (tûmôh) sêrhât, *or* tû sêrhâtmôh?. |
| (From whom) did he buy rice? | âmâ (tûkûngmôh§) bûfai âmântâ? |
| (What) is in the house? | înâh (îmôh) âhôm? |
| (What) is the matter? | (îtômôh) âhôm *or* (itômônî)? |
| (These) trees are big | (âmâhaihi) tînghai âlin. |
| (Each one) will get four annas | (‖enkât, kâtî) sîkî mânrâng. |
| (How many) men are there? | mîrim (îdôr môh) âhôm? |
| (Many) men have gone | mîrim (âtâm) âhôngtâ. |
| There is (nobody) in the village | kûâh (tûtê âhômmâhai).¶ |
| (How many) have gone? | (îdôrmôh) âfêtâ? |
| (How many) tigers did you see? | kâmgêï (îdôrmôh) âmûtâ?* |

## VERBS.

### Active.

| | |
|---|---|
| The men (have cut) the paddy | mîrimhai bûhôm (âtâ). |
| Men and women (live) in the village | mîrimhai, nûvenghai kûâh [âhômên (âhômtê=living, *or* âhôm=live]. |
| He (goes) to-morrow | âmâ nâgtûk (fêrâng).† |
| Are you (eating)? | nâng bû (ânêgmôh)? |
| Do you (sleep) in thehouse? | înâh nâng (ne) (jâlênmôh)? |
| Do you (live) in the hills? | lâmtûngâh (*or* hâsôk)‡ âhômmôh, *or* âhômên môh. |

---

* "Ârôtpûhai" means literally the "runners away."

† "The man seen by you," *lit.*

‡ "The coming men" have returned, *lit.*

§ "Tûkûngmôh" takes the place of "tûmôh, âtâ," "from whom?" it is idiomatic.

‖ *Lit.* "one: one, "= "each one."

¶ "Tûtê âhômmâhai" is very idiomatic, it signifies "there is not one who remains."

* The "you" is here understood.

† *Lit.*, "will go."

‡ "Hâsôk" means "in the hills" in contradistinction to "in the plains."

| | |
|---|---|
| I (had gone) away | gê (tinâ âfêtâ). |
| Are they (cutting) grass? | âmâhai (lhôî âjûnmôh) ? |
| He (went) to the plains yesterday | âmâ phaiâh (âfêtâ), mîâhu. |
| They have all (come) to the village | âmâhai ârêngâh kûâh (âhôngtâ). |
| Will you (cut) the *jhúms*? | nâng lôî (jûnrângmôh)?* |
| I (will bring) the men in the evening. | gê kôlôïâh mîrimhai (hông-jôïrâng). |
| Next month I (will send) them | gê tâkâtâh âmâhai (thîr-râng). |
| When are you (to give) the men? | nâng êtîgmôh mîrimhai (pê-râng) *or* (pêrôshê)? |
| They (will) all come | âmâhai ârêngâh (âhông-râng). |
| (Go) to the village now | âtûn kûâh (fêrô). |
| I (will go) there at once | gê âtûn shôshôn (fêrâng). |
| (If) you (go) you will be paid | nâng âfîentê shûm (mân-râng)†. |
| (Had) I (gone) it would have been well. | gê tînâ (âfêïntê âfêai) âsâ-tâ‡. |
| You (could) work. | nâng kâm (tôtêtâ). |
| He goes (to search) for deer | âmâ sâjûk (jôngrôshê âfê. |
| (Having arrived) I shall stop | (gêtûngâh) gêhômrâng§. |

PASSIVE VOICE.

| | |
|---|---|
| Deer (are found) in the jungles | sâjûkhai râmâh (âhômlê). |
| They (are caught) in traps | âmâhai pûngâh (âshûmlê). |
| It (had been) shot with a gun | âmâ shêlailê (âkâptâ). |
| (Having been caught) I was punished | (âjailenjû) sâjâr âmântâ‖. |
| On account of the child I (was not sent) | naitê ânîâh gê (mâ) (nâtîr-mâk).¶ |

* "Jûnrôshê" takes the place of "jêmrôshê," "to cut" when referring to *jhúm* and jungle-cutting generally.

† "Shûm mânrâng," *lit.*, "will get money."

‡ "Âfêai" is used for "had I gone; if I had gone:" "âsâtâ," "it was good," lit., and not "it would have been well."

§ This sentence is peculiarly idiomatic; "gê," "I," is attached to the verb "tûngrôshê," "to arrive," and the word for "to," in," *i.e.*, "âh," is affixed to the root of the verb; we thus have a compound of pronoun, verb, and loc: sign "âh;" the only translation this compound is susceptible of is "I arrive to," or "arriving to."

‖ *Lit.*, received punishment.

¶ "Âtîr" is the root of the verb; the "n" is added for euphony's sake.

### NEGATIVE VERBS.

| | |
|---|---|
| He (comes not) from the village | âmâ kûâtâ (âhôngmâk). |
| I (will not go) | gê (âfĕnônî).* |
| Are you (not going) out ? | nâng kôlaiâh [(â) fĕmâkmôh] ? |
| They (will not arrive) | âmâhai (âtûngmâk). |
| I (could not get) the coolies | mîrim (âmănnônî). |
| It (will not) rain. | rû (âtômâk *or* rû âtônônî). |
| Is it (not raining) ? | rû (âtômâkmôh) ? |
| I (cannot go) this morning | gê âvîm jingâh (âfĕnônî). |
| Can you (not go) now ? | âtûn, nâng (âfĕnônmôh) ?† |
| I (had not) a gun to shoot with | gêâh shêlai (âhômmâktâ). |
| (Had) they (not) guns ? | shêlai (ômâktâmôh) ?‡ |
| Why did they (not come) ? | îtômôh (âhôngmâk) ? |

Very often tense terminations are omitted when a verb is used in its negative form ; the sense in which the verb is intended to be used being gathered from the context.

### OTHER VERBS.

| | |
|---|---|
| He has (done nothing whatsoever) | âmâ (kâmîtê tômâk). |
| It is of the (very best) | âsâtâk (âsâôltâk). |
| He (is very ill) | (ânâbâk). |
| You are exceedingly bad | nâng shâlöîtâk. |
| It is exceedingly good | âsâtâk : âsâôltâk. |
| There is nothing to fear | êtêjîmâk. |
| It (is very large) | âmâ (âlinbâk).§ |
| This tree [is exceedingly tall (high)] | âmâtîng (ânshângbâk). |
| It (is quite close) | (ânaitêng). |
| It (is very far) | (âllâhbâk). |
| (Will you) (come back again) ? | nâng [(â) hôngnôgrângmôh] ? |
| I shall go again | gê âfĕnôgrâng. |
| (Have) they (gone back to the village) ? | âmâhai (kûâh âfĕnôg tâmôh) ? |
| You run back again | nâng âròtnôgrô. |
| Shoot again : fire again | âkâpnôgrô. |

* The negative is shown here by "I cannot go," instead of "will not."

† "Âfĕnonîmôh" sometimes appears in a curtailed form, the final "î" being omitted, "âfĕnônmôh."

‡ "Were there no guns ?" "they" understood.

§ The verb is all there is understood.

| | |
|---|---|
| Will you fire again? | nâng âkâpnôgrângmôh ? |
| (Is) the work (quite *or* entirely completed)? | kâm (apûmpûinâjöïtâmôh)? |
| They must go | âmâhai (â) fêrângănnî. |

## ADVERBS.

| | |
|---|---|
| You must come quickly | nâng âhôngenrângrô*ănnî. |
| How shall I go? | gê îtinmôh fêrâng ? |
| How will they come? | âmâhai îtinmoh âhôngrâng ? |
| There are only a few | âjintê, âjintê âhôm. |
| You walk slowly | nângmâ năfêâjâm.† |
| Do the work in this way | êhânghing kâm tôrô. |
| We will go to-day | gêni âvûn afêrâng. |
| He goes to-morrow | âmâ nâgtûk (â) fêrâng. |
| We will go in the morning | gêni jingâh âfêrâng. |
| It is below the hill | lâmtûng tângâh. |
| The village is above the river | kû dûìkông âsâkâh. |

## PREPOSITIONS, CONJUNCTIONS, INTERJECTIONS.

| | |
|---|---|
| I have come from the village | gê kûâtâ âhôngtâ. |
| Go to the village | kûâh fêrô. |
| I went up to the deer | gê sâjûkâh âfêtâ. |
| It is like a tiger | kâmgêî dôr. |
| On account of the rain I did not come | rûatôâh âhôngmâk.‡ |
| Because you did not come, you are punished | âhôngmâk jêâh (kânjû) sâjâr âmantâ (nământa). |
| He, therefore, left the village | âmâ ângkân kûâmâktâ. |
| Alas! he is dead | hê! (hai) âtitâ. |
| Hallo! come here | ôî! hôngrô. |
| Hush! he will hear | jông-nôrô enrîtrâng. |
| Well done! Bravo! | âsâ! âsâjîk! |

### *General conversation with a villager.*

| | |
|---|---|
| Where is your village? | nângkû kôtîngmôh? |
| How many houses are there? | în îdôrmôh âhôm? |
| There are forty | shôm mîlî âhôm. |

---

* "enrâng" is equivalent to "rât," quickly; quick.

† The "nă" is inserted for the sake of euphony, the sentence reads "your walk is slow."

‡ "kânjû" show cause, thus, "rû âtô kânjû," "because it rained *or* on account of rain," "kânjû" may also be said to take the place of "and so," *i.e.*, it rained "and so" I did not come (came not). "Kânjû" does not always appear, however, as in the sentence, which perhaps might be translated freely as "in the rain, I came not."

| | |
|---|---|
| Of these how many pay revenue? | îdôrmôh kâjânâ âpêk? |
| Thirty-five | shôm-tûm ringâh. |
| What (how much) do you pay per house? | înkât, kât îdôrmôh âpê? |
| Two rupees each house | inkât dârnî. |
| Is the land about you good? | ernêng âsâmôh? |
| Not very good: not very bad | shâbâkômmâk: âsâdê. |
| Last year we got plenty (much) | mîhîkûm âtâm âmântâ. |
| Are there many tigers? | kâmgêî âtâm âhômmôh? |
| Yes! we fear them greatly | âhôm gêni gejîbâk. |
| Do they carry off (seize) men? | mîrim kâmgêî âfâkmôh? |
| Yes! six men have been taken this year | mîrim (kûmîn) gărûk âfâktâ. |
| Have you no guns in the village? | kûâh shîlai âhômmôh?* |
| We have, but we cannot shoot the tiger. He is very cunning. | âhôm, kânjû âkâpnônî. Kâmgéî âfingbâktâ. |
| Your village must supply five maunds of rice | nângmâ kû bûfai maund ringâh pêrangennî. |
| Where shall we take the rice? | bûfai kôtîngmôh âtâkrâng? |
| Take it to Gonjong | Gonjongâh tâkrô. |
| Give the coolies to-morrow morning | nâgtûk jingâh mîrim pêrô. |
| How many coolies are required? | mîrim îdôrmoh nângrâng? |
| There is a puja in the village. | kûâh âsêrtâ. |
| How long will it last? | shûn îjâmôh *or* îdôrmôh tôrrang? |
| Five days | shûn ringâh. |
| What is your case | nângmâ jông imôh. |
| My rice has been stolen | gêmâ bûfai anrûktâ. |
| When? | îtigâhmôh. |
| Yesterday evening I caught the thief | mîjânâh enrû găjêlta. |
| Your case will be taken up to-morrow | nâgtûk nângmâ jông shîlrâng. |
| Bring all your people | ârêngah hôngjöîrô. |
| Are the *jhúms* burned? | lôi âhâltâmôh? |
| No! there is still a month left | âhâlmâk, tâkât bâkî âhôm. |
| Is your cotton good? | pât âsâmôh? |
| Yes, very good | âsâbâk. |
| What is the price a maund? | maund kât îdôr môh? |
| Four rupees | dâr mîlî. |

---

* *Lit.*, "are there any guns in the village?"

| | |
|---|---|
| Is there any shikar here ? | hîtingêh shâ âhômmôh? |
| Deer, tiger, and pig | sâjûk, kâmgêî, vôk âhôm. |
| Come out with me to-morrow to shoot deer | nâgtûk gêjânpui hôngro: sâjûk* kâprâng. |
| Are there any fish in this river | dûî kôngâh / dûî dûngah } gănâ âhômmôh. |
| Now there are a few | âtûn gîjînâ âhôm. |
| In the rains there are many | fûrâh âtâm âhôm. |
| Can you get them ? | âmântê; âmântêmôh?† |
| Will it rain to-day ? | âvûn rûtô râmgmôh? |
| No ! not this month | âmâ tââh rû âtômâk. |
| Send for your headman | gâlîm gôïrô (call). |
| There are two headmen | gâlîm ennî âhôm. |
| Send for both | ennî gôïrô. |
| Sir, one is ill | enkât ânâtâ. |
| Bring up the other | âdâng (mîdâng) hông jôïrô. |
| He is in the *jhúm*, but will return in the evening | lôiâh âhôm, kôlôïâh âhông nôgrâng. |
| Tell me when he comes | âhônglê jôngrô. |
| Have you a wife ? | daumâ âmantâmôh? |
| Yes : I married last year | mînîkûm daumâ âlâgtâ. |
| Where are your children ? | naitê hai kôtîng môh? |
| They are in the house | înâh âhôm? |
| Do they work ? | kâm âtô (âtômôh)? |
| Yes: a little (do a little) | âjin, âjin kâm âtô. |
| Do you eat opium ? | gânî âfâkmôh? |
| No: it is not our custom | âfâk (*or* âfâ) mâk: bâlâm nîmâk. |
| Are they Kacharis or Nágas ? | gâjârîmôh mîrông môh? |
| They are Kukis | Rangkholhai âhôm. |
| From what village ? | tûmôh kû *or* tûkûmôh?‡ |
| I do not know | gê têhai. |
| Come again in the evening | kôlôïâh âhôngnôgrô. |
| Bring the headman with you | gâlîm jân pûiâh hông jôïrô. |
| Is there any sickness in the village ? | kûâh ânâ âhôm môh ? |
| Three men have died this year. | kûmin§ mîrim entûm âtîtâ. |

* "sâjûk" refers to big deer, sambar. "Sâki" is a barking deer.

† "You" is understood.

‡ Either "tûmôhkû" or "tûkûmôh" is correct, but the latter is perhaps the more common.

§ "This year," "last year," are expressed by different words, "kûmîn," "mînîkûm."

| | |
|---|---|
| One died from cholera | enkât faibû âtâ* âtîtâ. |
| Were they young men? | âmâhai rûtârtê âjângrâng môh ?† |
| Yes: they were unmarried. | daumâ âlâmâk.‡ |
| Did they die in the plains or in the hills? | phaiâh âtîtâmôh hâsôkâh âtîtâ? |
| They died in the village | kûâh âtitâ. |
| When do you leave? | îtigmôh fêrâng? |
| Early to-morrow and return the next day. | nâgtûk jîngâh âfênogâh âhôngnôgrâng. |
| I have brought some plantains | gê môt âhông jôïtâ. |
| I can show some shikar | gê shâ ermûrâng. |
| There are deer and bear | sâjûk shâbôm âhôm. |
| We will go to the place later | lâgân gênî shôshôn fêrâng. |
| What work is your village doing this year? | kûmîn nângmâ kû îmôh kâm entô? |
| We are working on the road | lâmpûî (âh) kâm âtô (gâtô). |
| On which road? | kôlâmmôh?§ |
| On the old road | lâpui mîrûâh. |
| You must work for two months | tânî kâm tô-râng gäni.\|\| |
| What is your mauzadár's name? | môzârî ermîng îmânî? |
| Have you seen the Sahibs? | sâbhai âmûtâ môh? |
| Cut the grass and posts now | naidî chôpûî âtûn âtrô. |
| Bring some fowls and eggs | âr ârdûî hôngjôirô. |
| There are none in my house | gêmâ înâh ô-mâk. |
| Men are wanted for soldiers | sêpâî kâm tôrôshê mîrim âjông. |
| How many gods are there? | pâtînhai îdôrmoh âhôm? |
| Three or four and many evil spirits. | entûm milî âhom, pâtîn shâmâk âtâm. |
| On sickness do you sacrifice to the good or the bad spirits? | ânâlê (ânâ âhômlê) âsâ pâtîn âtô shâmâk pâtîn âtômôh? |
| In sickness to the bad | ânâ âhômlê¶ shâmâk pâtîn âtô. |

* "faibû" means, *lit.*, "wind." Cholera is believed by the Kukis to be caused by a bad wind.

† The verb understood.

‡ *Lit.*, "they had not wives."

§ Idiomatic, the root of "kôtîngmôh," "where," is prefixed to the root of "lâmkûî," "road," thus "kôlâm"="where road," "what road," or "which road."

|| *Lit.*, "it is necessary you will work."

¶ *Lit.*, "being ill."

| English | Rangkhol |
|---|---|
| We offer to the good gods on planting our paddy | fâjî* âlinglê âsâ pâtin âtô.† |
| When a man dies, what is done with the body? | mîrim âtî ârûôkâh îtinmôh entô âtô? |
| It is always burned | ânîtin âhâl (gănhâl.) |
| Where do you burn it? | kôtîngmôh âhâl? |
| Near the villages | kôkôlâ.‡ |
| Why not in the village? | îtômôh kûâh âhâlmâk? |
| It is not customary | (â) bâlâm nîmâk (âmâk). |
| How many wives can a man have? | mîrim enkât daumâ îdôrmôh âmâwai? |
| One only | enkât vai. |
| Can he leave his wife? | âmâ daumâ mâtênmôh? |
| No: he cannot leave her | mâtên nonî (nonîng).§ |
| Who inherits the property? | tûmôh nênûm âmân? |
| The sons only will get | ânaiîng vai mânrang. |
| Do the daughters receive nothing? | ânainûpâng ânêmâkmôh ? |
| They only get the ornaments of the mother | ânû {kûrdôi / tôiâhlê} vâi âmân. |
| The eldest son, if there are several, gets the property | âtâm âhômlê ûlînôlpâ‖ nênûw âmân. |
| The younger sons get a little | naipângtâk âjîn âmân. |
| What property have Rangkols? | Rângkhôl haiâh îmoh nênûw âhôm? |
| They have mithan, pigs, goats, and fowls. | shîl shêloi, vôk, gêl, âr âhôm. |
| How many mithan does a man keep? | mîrim enkât shîl îdôrmôh annê? |
| Five or six, sometimes ten or more. | ringáh, gărûk îtig îtig shômkât âhôm. |
| Are they killed for pujas ? | pâtîn âtôâh¶ ântât môh ? |
| A few are killed | enkât, ennî (one, two=a few) ântât. |
| What animals are used for pujas ? | pâtîn âtôâh îmôh antât ? |

* "fâjî" is the name for seed-paddy; "bûhôm" is ordinary paddy.

† "pâtîn âtô," *lit.*, "we do to god," "kill to god," &c.

‡ Idiomatic, "near the village."

§ "nônî" is sometimes pronounced "nôning."

‖ "ûlînôl" is the comparative: this is the commoner form, but it is correct to say "ûlintâk," "eldest."

¶ The "n" is inserted after the "â" for the sake of euphony.

| | |
|---|---|
| Pigs, goats, and fowls | vôk, gêl, âr. |
| Was your village formerly in the plains? | tînâ (tînâh {nângnî / nângmâ} kû phaiâh âhômtâmôh (hômmôh)? |
| We have always been in the hills. | ânîtin hâsôkâh âhôm.* |
| Are you afraid of the plains? | phai gănjîmôh (nâjîmôh)? |
| Down there we always get ill (are ill). | phaiâh ânîtin gânnâ.† |
| Cholera or small-pox? | faibû, zipôhmôh? |
| Do you work on tea-gardens? | bâgîsâ âh kâm âtômôh? |
| Never: not even when we go down in the cold weather. | âtômâk: kôsâlâh âfêlê kâm âtômâk. |
| Can you speak the plains language? | phaijông nâng rît môh? |
| A little | âjîn. |
| I can speak Kachari well | gâjârî jông âsâtê {gânrît / ârît}. |
| Which is the harder? | tû jôngmôh‡ antâk? |
| The plains language | phaijông antâk. |
| Is the Nága language difficult? | mîrông jông antâk môh? |
| It is not | antâk mâk (*or* âôl)§. |
| You can learn it in a year. | kûm enkâtâh enrîhrâng. |
| Will you teach me? | nâng erjûirâng môh? |
| For six months I will | tâ gărûk erjûirang. |
| Afterwards I shall have *jhúm* work. | lâgânâh lôî kâm âhômrâng‖ |
| Good: come to me from to-morrow. | âsâ: nâgtûkâtâ hôngrô. |
| My complaint is against the headman of my village. | gêmâ dôrkâst, gêmâ kûâh gâlîm âermîng¶ âhôm. |
| Three days ago he got an order to supply ten men for road work. | shûn tûm ânîtâ âmâ lâmpûî kâm âtôrôshê mîrim shômkât âpêrôshê hûkûm âmântâ. |

* *lit.*, "we are always in the hills."

† "gânnâ," idiomatic, meaning "we get ill;" "ânâ" is illness in a general sense.

‡ *lit.*, "which speech."

§ "âôl," "easy;" "ântâk," "hard;" "antâk mâk," "not hard."

‖ *lit.*, "will be jhúm work."

¶ The "â" preceding," "erming" "name," is inserted for euphony.

| | |
|---|---|
| This year I have done ten days' work, and other men should be taken. | kûmîn gê shûn shôm kâm gê entôtâ (gê âtôtâ): mîdâng âtôrôshê*. |
| I told him this, but he did not listen. | âmââh gê âtêtâ, kânjû gê jông lâmâk†. |
| I wish for a paper (order) excusing me from work. | gê mâp mânrâng lêkâ gêjông.‡ |
| You have done five days' work. | nâng shûn ringâh kâm âtôtâ. |
| On the ten being completed, you will be let off. | shûmshôm âjôïlê mâp mânrâng |
| Your name has been entered, and I will call in the head-man. | nângmâ ermîng âshûïtâ gê gâlîm gôïrâng. |
| Go back now at once to the work. | âtûn kâmâh fênôgrô. |
| I have come to say our villages are cutting their paddy. | gê âhông kânjû gênî kûmîhai âtûn bû (an) ât. |
| They ask for eight days' leave. | shûn gărit mâp {gêjông§. / gênjông.} |
| Their work will be finished in eight days. | shûn gărit kâm âjôïrâng. |
| Half the men will do road work and half will remain in the village. | mîrim âjimrip lâmpûî kâm (â) tôrâng ; âjimrip kûâh (â) hômrâng. |
| The men in our village are having a dispute. | gênî kûmîhai enjông âtâmtâ. |
| Six years ago there were only ten houses, and the waste land was sufficient. | kûm gă-rûk ânîtâ, în shôm âhôm, râm âtâm âhômta‖. |
| Now we have twenty houses, and there is no spare land. | âtûn în shômennî âhôm kânjû râm ernêng¶ ômâk. |

* "mîdâng âtôrôshê" for others to do: "others should do."

† "gê jông lâ mâk," *lit.*, "my speech (my words) did not accept."

‡ *lit.*, "to get pardon: (in order I will pardon) a paper (order) I ask for."

§ The "they" and "I" in these sentences is shown in a peculiar manner, the pronoun being prefixed to the verb; "gê," "I" "gêjông;" "I ask," "gên," short of "gênî," we, "gênjông," "we ask them," are colloquial forms, and the pronouns may be kept distinct without changing the sense.

‖ "râm âtâm âhômtâ," "there was much jungle" (waste land).

¶ "râm ernêng," "jungle land."

| | |
|---|---|
| The village next to ours is small, and they have much land. | gêni dûikôlkû,* âjintâ kânjû âmâhai ernêng âtâm. |
| We want to *jhúm* on some of it. | gêni ârni (âmâ) ernêngâh enrât-rôshê† gênhi. |
| We ask that some of the land be made over to us. | gêni gênhi âmâ râm gêni pêrâng‡. |
| The quarrel has now been going on for four years. | âni jông kûm mîlî ânitâ. |
| I will call in both village "galims." | gê kûnî gâlîmhai gôirâng. |
| With them all the witnesses must come. | âmâhai (âni) jân pûiâh ârêng âhôngrâng âni. |
| Five days from to-day the case will be settled. | âvûmâtâ shûm ringâh [môkôdômâh (dévân)§ âtôrâng.] |
| Each will point out the boundaries. | enkât kât râmrî ermûrâng. |
| What are your names? | nângnî ermîng îmôh? |
| Name of the village? | kû ermîng îmôh? |
| The "galim's" name? | gâlîmhai ermîng îmôh? |
| How many houses were there last year? | mînî kûm în îdôrmôh âhômtâ? |
| This man married my daughter. | âmâ mîrim gêmâ ânai âlâktâ. |
| By our custom he should pay forty rupees. | gêni bâlâm âtâ gê dâr shômmîlî mânrâng‖ [âmâ pîrâng âni]. |
| After the marriage he gave me two goats and a pig. | daumâ âlâktâ gêmâ gêl ennî kânjû vôk enkât âpêtâ. |
| He said in three days he would pay twenty rupees. | âmâ âtîtâ shûn entûm îm shôm ennî âpêrâng. |
| Every month he says he will pay, but he does not do so. | tâ kât, tâkât âmâ âti shân pêrâng, kânju pêmâk. |
| It is five months since the marriage took place | daumâ âlaktâ ringâh âhôm. |
| I cannot get the money | gê shôm mântêmâ ŭng.¶ |

* "dûi kôlkû," "neighbouring village."

† "envât-rôshê," "to jhúm."

‡ "*Lit.*, "we ask their land will be given to us."

§ "dêvân" is the Kuki "case," "dispute," "dêvân lôrô," "to settle cases:" "môkôdômâh," however, commonly used.

‖ "He should pay" is changed to "I will get;" in this sentence "he should pay," "âmâ pêrangâni," is in brackets.

¶ "mântêmâ ŭng" is idiomatic.

| | |
|---|---|
| Have the galims decided on this matter? | gâlîmhai dêvân âtôtâmôh ? |
| Once they held council | voïkât âtôtâ (dêvâm âtôtâ). |
| What did they say ? | îmôh âtîtâ ? |
| They said the man must pay five rupees each month. | âmâhai âtî, tâkât, tâkât shôm dâr ringâh pêrâng.* |
| How many months ago is this? | tâ îdôrmôh âhôm ? |
| Two months | tâ ennî† (*or* tânî). |
| Where is he now ? | âtûn âmâ kôtîngmôh âhôm. |
| He is in the village ? | âmâ kûâh âhôm. |
| Call him in during the next three days. | shûn tûm shûngâh (âmâ) gôïrô. |
| I have brought in four tiger's skins. | gê kâmgêï vûn mîlî âhông jôïtâ. |
| I ask for a reward for each one. | enkât enkât âmân‡ ânjông. |
| In the village we have two leopards' skins. | kûâh kâmgêï vûm âjînjât ennî âhôm. |
| I will bring them in afterwards. | lâgânâh gê âhôngjôïrâng. |
| All the animals were caught in traps. | shâ ârêng (âh) fûngâh (gâr) âlût gênjêl§. |
| The big one had carried off man goats and pigs from the village. | âlîmpâ, gêl, vôk âtâm kûâlâ âjôitâ (âfâktâ)‖. |
| He entered the village at night. | jânâh kûâh âlût (tâ). |
| I return to-day to the village. | gê âvûm kûâh âfênôgrâng. |
| You will be paid twenty-five rupees for each tiger's skin. | nâng kâmgêï vûn kât enkât shôm ennî dâr ringâh (â) mânrâng. |
| For the leopards you will receive five rupees each. | kâmgêï ajînjât, dâr ringâh dâr ringah mânrâng. |
| How many animals did the tiger kill ? | shâ îdôrmôh kâmgêï âfâktâ ? |

* "Pêrâng," *lit.*, "will pay," in this case means "must pay" as well.

† "Ennî," "two," sometimes appears in a shorter form, "nî."

‡ "Amân," *lit.*, price.

§ "gâr âlût gênjêl," "entering (having entered) the traps we caught."

‖ "âfâktâ," "devoured," used in reference to beasts of prey.

| | |
|---|---|
| Many: ten pigs and five goats. | âtâm: vôk shôm kât, gêi ringah. |
| Did you ever shoot a tiger? | nâng kâmgêi âtâttâ môh ?* |
| Once | Voïkât. |
| You will go back this evening. | nâng âvûn kôlôiâh fênôgrâng. |
| Stay here now | âtûn hîting (â) hômrô. |
| I gave this man twenty rupees. | âmâ mîrimhî shômnî găpêgtâ.† |
| I gave the money to buy a "mithan" for me. | gê shîl erjaâh‡ shôm găpê (g) tâ. |
| I gave it four months ago. | tâ mîlî gê âpêtâ (găpêtâ). |
| Seven days ago he returned to the village. | shûn sârî âmâ kûâh âhông-nôgtâ. |
| I said "where is my mithan?" | gê âtîtâ "gêmâ shîl kôting-môh?" |
| He said "what mithan?" | âmâ âtîtâ "îmôhshîl?" |
| The one you were to buy | âmâ nâng erjarôshê âfêtâ.§ |
| I gave you twenty rupees | gê nângmâ shôm ennî {âpêtâ / găpêtâ.} |
| He said "I never got the rupees." | âmâ âtîtâ "gê shôm âmân-mâk." |
| I have several witnesses | gêmâ sâkîhai âtâmâhôm. |
| Are they of your village? | nângmâ kûmôh? |
| Of my village and of his | gêmâ mâ kû; âmâ kûhai. |
| His brother was with him | âmâ ûpâ jânpûi âhômtâ. |
| What time of the day did he receive the money? | mîsâ îdôrmôh‖ âmâ shôm âmân-tâ? |
| At 12 o'clock. | mîsâ ending.¶ |
| The Râja of our village has sent me. | gênî kû rêng gêtîrtâ. |
| He is ill and cannot come | âmâ ânâtâ: âhôngtêmâk. |
| I am his minister (montri) | gê âmâ "môntrî" âhôm. |

* "âtâttâ," "destroyed," used in the sense of firing and killing an animal.

† "găpêgtâ:" the "gă" is simply another form of "i," "gê;" "pêta" appears as pêgtâ: no rule can be quoted for this change; "pêtâ" is equally correct.

‡ "erjarôshê" is the infinitive of the verb; "erjaâh" is a verb with a substantive case-ending affixed: this form is rather rare.

§ *Lit.*, "the one to buy you went."

‖ *Lit.*, "mîsâ îdôrmôh," "what amount of sun?" "how stood the sun?"

¶ "mîsâ ending" is the term used for "mid-day," "twelve o'clock."

| | |
|---|---|
| My name is Nîrâ | gêmâ ermîng Nîrâ âtî.* |
| The Rája married three years ago. | kûm entûmtâ† âmâ daumâ âmântâ.‡ |
| He had two children | naipânghai ennî âmântâ. |
| Last year both these died | mînîkûm âtitâ§ (âmâhai ennî). |
| He has no other children | âdâng naipânghai ômâk. |
| A month ago, he married another wife. | tâkât ânîtâ, âmâ mîdâng (daumâ) âmântâ (âlâktâ). |
| The first wife and the present one are constantly fighting | mâtônâ daumâ, âtûnâh daumâ ânîtin ershûl. |
| The new wife is in the family way. | âtûnâh daumâ enraitâ. |
| The other is very angry | mîdâng âhâl-ôktâ.‖ |
| By our customs only one wife is allowed. | gênî bâlâm, daumâ enkât vai gênlâkai.¶ |
| The Rája has two | rêngâh ennî âhôm. |
| He wants a son | nai ângî. |
| The relations of the wives are very angry. | daumâhai anpûng â(n) hâlôktâ. |
| The relations of the first wife want to take her away. | mâtônâ gadaumâ âpûng (âshûnghôk) âmâ nëïrâng âti.* |
| The Rája wishes to keep both. | rêng ennî shêrang a(n) tî. |
| He asks your orders. | âmâ kûkûm ângî. |
| Where do the relations of the wives live ? | daumâhai anpûng kôtîngmôh âhômlê *or* (hônmôh âhom) ?† |
| In Taijol village | Taijôl kûâh âhôm. |
| The others in Haitu village | mîdânghai Haitû kûâh. |
| How far from here ? | hîtâkâh âtâî‡ îdôrmôh âllâh ? |

---

* "Nîrâ âtî," *lit.*, is "said Nira," the whole sentence literally "my name is said Nira (is called Nira)".

† "entûmtâ," "is there."

‡ *Lit.*, "It is three years he got a wife, *i.e.*, is married."

§ "Last year died," the "âmâhai ennî" is generally understood.

‖ "âhâl-ôktâ," "very angry ;" "ôk" signifies in this case "exceedingly :" "very."

¶ "gên," short of "gênî," "we :" sentence "one alone we allowed (or can) marry."

* Here "want to take her away" appears literally as "say they will take away."

† "kônmôh," short of "kotingmôh," "where."

‡ The regular form of "hîtâkâh âtâî ;" "from here," is "hiting âtâ."

| | |
|---|---|
| Two days' journey | shûn nî lâm.* |
| Can they walk ? | âmâ âfêtîmôh ? |
| Yes: all are young (not old) | lâtârmak (âtârmâk). |
| Next month the Rája will come. | tâtârâh† rêng fêrâng. |
| He is old | âmâ târpâ. |
| His name is Paku | ermîng Pâkû âtî. |
| One man of our village has killed another | gêmkûâh mîrim enkâtîn enkât âtâttâ. |
| The day before yesterday (the) two men left the village. | mîjânpê mîrim ennî kû âtâ afêtâ. |
| They went to the river Langting. | Lângtîng dûĭkôngâh âfêtâ. |
| They went in the early morning. | âmâ jîngâh âfêtâ. |
| They reached the river at 4 o'clock (afternoon). | âmâ bôsûrûpâh‡ âtungtâ. |
| They caught a great deal of fish. | gănâ âtâm, âtâm§ âmântâ. |
| At night they slept in an old hut. | jâwâh înmîrûâh âjâltâ. |
| One man had a gun | enkât shêlai âhômtâ. |
| In the morning he heard some elephants. | âmâ jingâh shaipui anrîttâ. |
| There was one big male | âjâl âlînpâ enkât.‖ |
| This male he fired at and killed. | âjâlâh shêlai ankâplê âtâttâ. |
| The other man saw him. | mîdângîn âmû.¶ |
| He said he would report the case to Gunjong. | âmâ Gônjônga jông entûnrâng* âtîtâ. |
| The owner of the gun said "if you do I will shoot you." | shêlai jôngkû âtîtâ nîng-tînjû nâng tâtrâng.† |

* *Lit.*, "two days' road."

† Tâ târâh=tâ, "moon" ("month"); "târ" short of "âtâr," "new;" "âh," "in," *or* "at," literally "at the new moon or month."

‡ "bôsûrûp" is the term for the day between 3 and 5 p.m. (afternoon).

§ "âtâm, âtâm," *lit.*, "much : much"="very much."

‖ The verb "âhôm" understood.

¶ "amûtâ" may be used.

* "jông entûnrâng," "will give the word."

† "tâtrâng," to shoot, kill, destroy, &c.

| | |
|---|---|
| The other replied "I am not afraid." | mîdâng âtîtâ "gê jîmâ (jîmâ-hông). âkâpâh* |
| The owner of the gun then fired and killed the other. | shêlai (â) jôngkû mîrim âtâttâ. |
| We have seized him | gênî âmâ anjêltâ. |
| He says he killed the man | âmâ âtî mîrim âtâtâ. |
| Where is the gun ? | shêlai kôtîngmôh ? |
| It will be brought in by this evening. | avûm kölôiâh âhông jôirâng. |
| Is it a Government gun ? | Sôrkâr shêlai âhômmôh. |
| Yes: a Government | Sôrkâr shêlai âhôm |
| Put it in the guard | gârdâh pêrô. |
| Bring up the man to-morrow early in the morning. | nâgtûk mîrim hôngjôirô (jingâh). |
| You must all come | nângnî ârêngâh fêrang. |

Every language may be said to have written and colloquial or conversational forms of speech.

In the foregoing sentences the writer has adopted the conversational form, partly to show how the words undergo various changes when brought into use in a sentence or sentences, and partly because this form would be the most useful to a student of the language, or to travellers passing through the hills inhabited by Kukis.

The purely grammatical forms can easily be made up, from the vocabulary and the rules, by any one. These latter forms, of course, are understood by the people, and are all that is needed; at the same it is desirable, the writer thinks, to show how various words are curtailed and added to in ordinary village talk, the meaning and force being much the same as that assigned to the full word.

The reader will see from the foregoing sentences that case-endings are as often as not omitted in talking, that the singular form answers for the plural, and that often, for the sake of euphony, syllables and letters are affixed.

The sentences have been in some cases translated into idiomatic Kuki, that is to say, the Kuki meaning for each English word has not been taken and a sentence formed, but the way the sentence would or should appear in the language is shown. The foot-notes give the *literal* meaning in English of the phrases.

* "Akâpâh," *lit.*, in shooting, or by shooting.

## VOCABULARY.

In the vocabulary most of the words in every-day use will be found, and also the greater number of those used in the foregoing sentences and reading lessons.

### A.

| | |
|---|---|
| A *or* an | enkât. |
| Abode | hômmûn. |
| Absent | ômâk. |
| Abuse (to) | jôngshâmâk. |
| Acid | âtûr. |
| Afoot | nîkêâh. |
| After | ennûng. |
| Air | faibu. |
| Alike | îdôrkât, mûnkât. |
| All | ârêngâh. |
| Alone | enkât. |
| Angry (to be) | bâlroshê. |
| Antler | ârkî |
| Arm | kût. |
| Ashamed (is) | anjâktâ. |
| Ashes | mêkû. |
| Assault (to) | ershûlshê. |
| At | âmâhin. |
| Aunt | gapuînâk.* |
| Axe | rhê. |

### B.

| | |
|---|---|
| Babe | naitê |
| Bachelor | daumalâlâmâk. |
| Back | rûöng |
| Bad | shâmâk. |
| Bag | mârsâ. |
| Baggage | nênûn. |
| Bamboo | rômai. |
| Banana | môt. |
| Bark (to) | enrâmrôshê. |
| Basket | rêl. |
| Bat | bâk. |
| Bathe (to) | ershîlrôshê. |
| Bazar | bâjâr. |
| Be (to) | hômrôshê. |
| Bead | ertê. |
| Beam | mîling. |
| Bear | shâvom. |
| Beard | nêrkâmûl. |
| Beast | shâ. |
| Beat (to) | jêmrôshê. |
| Bed | jâlmûl. |
| Bee | kûî. |
| Before | înmân. |
| Begin (to) | tôroshê. |
| Behind | ennûng. |
| Believe (to) | shônrôshê. |
| Belly | ping. |
| Betel | pânbû. |
| Big | âlîn. |
| Bird | âr. |
| Bite (to) | âshêrôshê. |
| Bitter | ânrâng. |
| Black | âvûm. |
| Blame (to) | tûtûmôh shâloî rôshê.† |
| Blind | mijô. |
| Blood | âtî. |
| Boar | vôkjâl. |
| Boat | êrgông. |
| Body | âtâk. |
| Bone | ârû. |
| Book | lâkâ. |
| Born | âshûoktâ. |
| Boy | naipâng. |
| Brave | âhai. |
| Bridge | erkâl. |

* Mother's younger sister.

† This the query "who to blame?"

Bring (to) hôngiôïrôshê.
Brother kâûpâ.
Bud ârâ.
Buffalo shêloî.
Bury (to) pûmrôshê.
But kânjû.
Buy (to) erjarôshê.
By ânnâï.

C.

Calf sêrhâttê.
Call (to) gôirôshe.
Camp erbûk.
Cane etîng.
Cash shûm.
Cat mêng.
Catch (to) jêlrôshê.
Centre âlaitâk.
Cheap (is) andoïtâ.
Chest milûng
Child naitê-naipâng.
Cholera faibû.
Climb (to) lûïrôshê.
Cloth pûn.
Cock ârkông.
Cold âdai.
Collect (to) pâlrôshê.
Comb sâmtî
Come (to) hôngrôshê
Complete (to) âjôïrôshê..
Converse (to) jôngrôshê.
Cord mînâng.
Count (to) têprôshê.
Cow serhât.
Customary (â) bâlâm.
Cut (to) jêmrôshê.

D.

Dance (to) lâmrôshê.
Dark âjîn.
Daughter nâinûpâng.
Day shûn.
Daybreak jîngâh (mîsâ âshûok.)
Dead (is) âtîtâ.
Deaf mîgúr âshêt.
Dear âholû.
Deepântûk.
Deer sâjûk.
Desire (to) îjôngrô.
Devil pâtînshâmâk.
Die (to) âtîrôshê.
Different âdâng.
Dirt sârok.
Dish jairbêl.
Distant âllâh.
Distress kôpûr.
Do hâ(to)tôrôshê.
Dog ûï.
Drunk jûenrûïtâ.
Duck râtôk.
Dumb jôngtêmâk.
Dung êk.
Dwell (to) âhômrôshê.

E.

Each enkât, enkât.
Ear migûr.
Earth ernêng.
Earthquake ningnû.
Ease âtâkâhôï.
East mîsâ âshûok.
Eat (to) âfâkrôshê.
Egg ârdûî.
Eight garît.
Elbow kî.
Empty âkôrông.
Enter (to) âlûrôshê.
Equal mûnkât.
Evening kôlôïâh.
Ever ânîtin.

| | | | |
|---|---|---|---|
| Every | kât, enkât. | Eye | mît. |
| Extraordinary (is) | gâmângtâ. | Eyebrow | mîtmûl. |
| | | Eyelid | mîtkôï. |

F.

| | | | |
|---|---|---|---|
| Face | mhai. | Flee (to) | ârôtrôshê. |
| Fall (to) | âtûkrôshê. | Flesh | mhê. |
| False | mîlâk. | Fly (to) | ârôtrôshê. |
| Famine | kôpûr. | Fog | shûmbûl. |
| Far | âllâh. | Foot | kê. |
| Fast | ârhât. | Force | ernâk. |
| Fat | âmêlâsâ. | Forehead | mîjâl. |
| Father (my) | gapâ. | Forest | tîngbîl. |
| Fear (to) | nâjîroshê. | Fowl | âr. |
| Feed (to) | rohairôshê. | Fresh | âtâr. |
| Fetch (to) | hôngjôïrôshê. | Frog | uîchôk. |
| Few | âjîn. | From | âtâ. |
| Fire | mê. | Fuel | tîng. |
| Fish | nâ. | Full (is) | âshîptâ. |
| Flat | phai: ânjôl. | Fur | cômê. |

G

| | | | |
|---|---|---|---|
| Garden | erhûn. | God | pâtîn. |
| Gate | enkâr. | Gold | râmgmâjâk. |
| Gave | âpêgtâ. | Good | âsâ. |
| Get (to) | âmânrôshê. | Got | âmântâ. |
| Girl | dôngmâtê. | Grasp (to) | jêlrôshê. |
| Give (to) | pêrôshê. | Grass | lhôï. |
| Go (to) | fêrôshê. | Great | âlîn. |
| Goat | gêl. | Gun | shêlai. |
| | | Gunpowder | bâkêr. |

H.

| | | | |
|---|---|---|---|
| Habit | bâlâm. | Hear (to) | anrîtrôshê. |
| Hail | rîl. | Heart | mîlûng. |
| Hair | sâm. | Heat | âlûm. |
| Half | âjîmrîb. | Heavy | ârîk. |
| Halfway | lâmjîmrîp. | Heel | gamîkông. |
| Hand | kût. | Here | hîtingâh. |
| Hard | ângâr. | Hew | jêmrô. |
| Hat | shâlkû. | High | âshê. |
| Have (to) | âmânrôshê. | Hill | lâmtûng. |
| Hawk | ermû. | Hit (to) | âtôkrôshê. |
| He | mî. | Horn | erkî. |
| Head | lû. | Hot | âlûm. |

House in. How ítînmôh.
Household înshûngkâtnû. Hungry pîngâjâm.
Husband (â) rûatâr.

I.

I gê (nî). Infant naitê.
Idiot entoh. Insect ergănê.
Ill ânâ. Inside ârîlâh.
In ârîlâh. Iron tîr.
Ivory shai-hâ.

J.

Jhúm loî. Jhúm (to) loîtorôshê.
Jungle râm.

K.

Keen angai. Kill (to) tâtrôshê.
Kick (to) ânrârôshê. Knee erkû.

L.

Labour kâm. Left vêtîng.
Lad rûtârtê. Leg âkê.
Lamp jâtîmê. Lemon mishêr.
Land ernêng. Letter lêkâ.
Language jông. Light (to) mêtôrôshê.
Large âlîn. Like mûnkât.
Laugh (to) âmîrôshê. Lime lôngjûn.
Leaf nâ-tîng-nâ Listen (to) enrîrôshê.
Leave (to) pairôshê. Little âjîn.
Leech ervôt. Look (to) enroshê.

M.

Mad entohtâ, envêt. Money shûm.
Male âzâl, basâl. Monkey jeông.
Man mîrim. Month (my) tâ.
Many âtâm. Moon tâ.
Market bâjâr. Morning jîngâh.
Match mêjî. Mosquito toïjûm.
Meat mhê. Mother ânû.
Meet (to) ârtongrôshê. Mouse mîjû.
Milk ernûtûï. Mouth múr.
Mine gênî. Much âtâm.

N.

Naked dîrbûi. Nephew shûmshûök.
Name er-mîng. Nest ârbû.
Needle shimpui Net lên.

| | | | |
|---|---|---|---|
| New | âtar. | Noon | mîsâ ending. |
| Night | jân. | Nose | nâr. |
| No | ômâk. | Nothing | entê-ômâk. |
| Now | âtûn. | | |

O.

| | | | |
|---|---|---|---|
| Oath | kômâ. | Orange | sômôtôrai. |
| Old | âmîrû. | Orphan | naifrâ. |
| One | enkât. | Owner | âjôngpû. |
| Opium | gânî. | Ox | sêrhât. |

P.

| | | | |
|---|---|---|---|
| Paddy | bûhôm. | Pig | vôk. |
| Paid (to be) | pêrâng. | Pigeon | pêrbâlî. |
| Paid | pêtâ. | Plantain | môt. |
| Papa | âpâ. | Play (to) | erdai. |
| Paper | lêkâ. | Poor | enrïng. |
| Pardon (to) | mâp. | Potato | bâl. |
| Pay (to) | pêrôshê. | Pregnant | enrai. |
| Piece | kûtkâng hât. | Pull (to) | gairôshê. |

Q.

| | | | |
|---|---|---|---|
| Quarrel (to) | ângêrshûl. | Quick | râtrô. |
| Quiet | enrûkâtên. | Quickly | râtrô. |

R.

| | | | |
|---|---|---|---|
| Race | jâdî. | Rich | erjông. |
| Rage (to) | âhâlrôshê. | Right | jângting. |
| Rain | rû. | Ripe (is) | âmîntâ. |
| Rája | rêng. | River | dûîkûng. |
| Rat | mîjû. | Road | lâmpûî. |
| Recover (to) | dâmrôshê. | Rob (to) | enrû rôshê. |
| Red | âsên. | Rock | lûng. |
| Return (to) | âhôngnôgrôshê. | Rod | erköipêr. |
| Rhinoceros | gôndâ. | Root | erjûng. |
| Rib | gâng. | Rope | mînâng. |
| Rice | bûfai. | Run (to | ârôtrôshê. |

S.

| | | | |
|---|---|---|---|
| Sacrifice | pâtintô. | Say | âtêrô. |
| Said | âtîtâ. | Sealing-wax | sâhâ. |
| Sâlâm | jûbai. | Search (to) | jôngrôshê. |
| Salt | mîjî. | See (to | enrôshê. |
| Same | dôr, dôr. | Seed | âr-rû. |
| Sap | annai. | Sense | bûdî. |
| Sat | tôîrô, tôîtâ. | Separate | âdâng. |

| | | | |
|---|---|---|---|
| Serpent | mîrûl. | So | îdôr. |
| Seven | sîrî. | Sow | entêkrô. |
| Shame | enjâk. | Speak (to) | jôngrôshê, âtî-rôshê. |
| Sheep | bêlrâ. | | |
| Shoot (to) | kâprôshê. | Spear | ôfê. |
| Shot | kâptâ. | Speech | jông. |
| Shut (to) | enkârôshê. | Spoke | jôngtâ. |
| Silk | elüng. | Stand | nîrô. |
| Silver | shûm. | Star | ârshî. |
| Sing (to) | lâjâk. | Stone | lûng. |
| Sister | sângnû. | Strength | ernâk, ârhât. |
| Six | ga-rûk. | Strike (to) | jêmrôshê. |
| Skin | âvûn. | Sugar | chînî. |
| Sky | ervân. | Sun | misâ. |
| Slave | shûök. | Sweet | ertân. |
| Sleep (to) | jâlrôshê. | Sweep | empîrô. |
| Slow | arhâtmâk. | Sweet | âtûï. |
| Small-pox | rhîpô. | Swim (to) | elhîrôshê. |

## T.

| | | | |
|---|---|---|---|
| Table | lûkâmtê. | Tie (to) | kîtrôshê. |
| Tail | argănê. | Tiger | kâmgêï. |
| Take (to) | lârôshê. | Tired | âshôltâ. |
| Talk (to) | jôngrôshê. | To | âh. |
| Tall | ârshâng, âshê. | Tobacco | dûmâ. |
| Tame (is) | âgănâmtâ. | Tobacco-pipe | dômbêl. |
| Tea | sâ. | To-day | âvûn. |
| Tell (to) | jongrôshê. | Together | jânpûî. |
| Tender | ârnöî. | Told | âjôngtâ. |
| There | shôshôn. | To-morrow | nâgtûk. |
| Thin | âkông. | Tongue | mêlê. |
| Thing | nênûn. | To-night | âvûnjân. |
| Thirsty | dûî enrâl. | Top | sâgtîng. |
| This | âmâhî. | Toucan | vâpûl. |
| Thorn | ellhing. | Track | ânûng. |
| Thousand | rêjâkât. | Trap | fûng. |
| Throat | rîng. | Tree | tîng. |
| Throw (to) | pairôshê. | Tribe | jât. |
| Thumb | kûpûî. | True | âdîk. |
| Thus | âîdôr, hîdôrhî. | Trust (to) | gărnai. |

## U.

| | | | |
|---|---|---|---|
| Uncle | gâpâtêr. | Understand | găn-rît, ânrit. |
| Under | tângtîng. | | |

## V.

| | |
|---|---|
| Vegetable | ân. |
| Vein | ârtârûî. |
| Village | kû. |

## W.

| | |
|---|---|
| Wait (to) | nîng-nâgrôshê. |
| Walk (to) | kâljöîrôshê. |
| Wander (to) | kûlâfêrôshê. |
| Want (to) | âhgănîrôshê. |
| War | râl. |
| Warn | âlûm. |
| Water | dûi. |
| Wax | kôîlû. |
| Way (road) | lâmpûî. |
| Wed (to) | daumâ lârôshê. |
| Weed (to) | enjunrôshê. |
| Weigh (to) | vârâng. |
| Wet (is) | âdûita |
| What | îmôh. |
| When | îtîgmôh. |
| Where | kôtîngmôh. |
| Who | tumôh. |
| Whose | tûmôhnî. |
| Why | îmânî. |
| Widow | mêtai |
| Widower | dângkông. |
| Wife | daumâ. |
| Wind | faibû. |
| Wish (to) | êmôh injông-rôshê. |
| Wonderful (is) | gâmângtâ. |
| Work | kâm. |
| Work (to) | kâm tôrôshê. |
| Write (to) | shûirôshê. |
| Writer | lêkâpû. |

## Y.

| | |
|---|---|
| Year | kûm. |
| Yes | ôh. |
| Yesterday | mîâhn. |
| You | nâng. |
| Yours | nângmâ. |

## NUMERALS.

| | |
|---|---|
| One | enkât. |
| Two | ennî. |
| Three | entûm. |
| Four | mîlî. |
| Five | ringâh. |
| Six | gărûk. |
| Seven | sârî. |
| Eight | gârit. |
| Nine | gûôk. |
| Ten | shôm. |
| Eleven | shômkât lêkât =10 and 1 &c., &c. |
| Thirty | shôm tûm (three tens). |
| Forty | shôm mîlî. |
| Fifty | shôm ringâh. |
| Sixty | shôm gărûk. |
| Seventy | shôm sârî. |
| Eighty | shôm gârit. |
| Ninety | shôm gûôk. |
| Hundred | rajâkât. |
| One thousand | shângkât. |

# Comparison of the Various Kuki Dialects and Lushai.

---

## COMPARISON OF THE DIALECTS OF THE KUKI LUSHAI TRIBES AND OF THE LANGUAGE KNOWN AS LUSHAI.

A vocabulary of 64 words in every-day use is given in each of the different dialects. From these vocabularies and the typical sentences a brief comparison can be made.

The vocabularies of the Rângkôls, Bêtês, and Sakâjaibs are given first, then those of the Jansens and Tadoïs, and lastly a Lushai vocabulary.

### VOCABULARY.

| *English.* | *Rangkôl.* | *Bêté.* | *Sakâjaib.* |
|---|---|---|---|
| Air | faibu | faibu | faibu. |
| All | ârêngâh | ârêngkân | ârêngîn. |
| Arm | kût | kut | kût. |
| Axe | rahî | rê | rê. |
| Bad | shâmâk | tâmâk | shâmâk. |
| Bamboo | rômai | rômai | rômai. |
| Bathe | ershîlrô (shê) | (t)ershîlrô | ershîlrô. |
| Bear | shâvom | îvom | âvôm. |
| Big | âlîn | âlîn | âlîn. |
| Bird | âr, âvâ | âr | âr. |
| Black | âvum | âvum | âvum. |
| Boat | argông | răgông | râgông. |
| Body | âtâk | âtâk | antâk. |
| Boy | naipâng | naipâng | naipâng. |
| Buy | erjarô (shê) | erjarô | erjarô. |
| Cock | ârkông ârpâ | ârkông | ârkông. |
| Come | hôngrô (shê) | hôngrô (shê) | hôngrô. |
| Cut | jêmrô (shê) | hêmrô | jêmrô. |
| Day | shûn | shûn | shûn. |
| Dead | âtîtâ | atîtâ | âtîjôï. |
| Dog | uï | uï | uï. |
| Earth | ernêng lê | rănêng | phîl. |
| Egg | ârduî | ârduï | ârduî. |
| Eye | mît | mît | mît. |
| Father | gapâ âpâ | âpâ | gâpâ. |
| Fire | mê | mê | mê. |
| Fish | nâh | engâ | nâ. |

| *English.* | *Râangkôl.* | *Bêtê.* | *Sakâjaib.* |
|---|---|---|---|
| Get | âmânrô (shê) | âmânrô | âmânrô. |
| Goat | gêl | gêl | gêl. |
| God | pâtîn | pâtîn | pâtîn. |
| Good | âsâ | âsâ | âsâ. |
| Gun | shêlai | shilai | shilai. |
| Hill | lâmtûng | lâmtûng | lâmtûng. |
| Husband | rûâtâr | klângrâl | rûtârtê. |
| Iron | tîr | tîr | tîr. |
| Jhúm | loï | loï | loï. |
| Kill | tâtrô (shê) | tâtrô | tâtrô. |
| Land | ernêng | ranêng | phîl. |
| Large | âlîn | âlîn | âlîn. |
| Man | mîrim | mîrim | mîrim. |
| Moon | tâ | tâ | tâ. |
| Mother (my) | ànû | ânû | ânû. |
| Night | jân | jân | jân. |
| Now | âtûn | âtûn | âtûn. |
| Old | âmîrû | âlûï | âmîrû. |
| Paddy | bûhôm | bûhûm | bûhûm. |
| Pig | vôk | vôk | vôk. |
| Rain | rû | rû | rû. |
| Red | âsên | âsên | âsên. |
| Rice | bûfai | afai | shishai. |
| River | dûîkûng | dûîkûng | dûîkûng. |
| Road | lâmpûî | lâmpûî | lâmpûî. |
| Run | ârôtrô (shê) | ârôtrô | êrôtrô. |
| Salt | mîjî | mîjî | mîjî. |
| Shoot | kâprô (shê) | kâprô | kâprô. |
| Speak | jôngrô (shê) | jôngrô | jôngrô. |
| Sun | mîsâ | mîsâ | mîsâ. |
| Tiger | kâmgêï | îkê | âkê. |
| Tobacco | dûmâ | dûmâ | dûmâ. |
| To-day | âvûn | âvûn | âvûn. |
| To-morrow | nâgtûk | nâgtûk | nângtûk. |
| Village | kû | kû | kû. |
| Water | dûî | dûî | dûî. |
| Work | kâm | kâm | kâm. |
| One | enkât | enkât | enkât. |
| Two | ennî | ennî | ennî. |
| Three | entûm | entûm | entûm. |
| Four | mîlî | mîlî | mîlî. |
| Five | ringâh | ringâh | ringâh. |
| Six | gărûk | gêrûk | ârûk. |

| | | | |
|---|---|---|---|
| Seven | sârî | sârî | sârî. |
| Eight | gărit | gărit | ârît. |
| Nine | guôk | guôk | âguôk. |
| Ten | shôm | shôm | shôm. |
| One hundred | rajâkât | rajâkât | râjâkât. |
| Two hundred | rajânî | rajanî | rajanî. |
| One thousand | shânkât | shângkât | shângkât. |

SENTENCES.

(1) *English.* Where is your village ?
*Rangkhol.* Nâng (mâ) kû kôtîngmôh?*
*Bêtê.* Nâng mâ kû (kâ) tâkâm?*
*Sakâjaib.* Nângmâ kû kônmôh?*

(2) *E.* Is the land good?
*R.* Ernêng âsâmôh?
*B.* Ernêng âsâmôh?
*S.* Phil âhôîmôh?

(3) *E.* Your village must supply five maunds of rice.
*R.* Nángmâ kû bûfai maund ringâh pêrâng ennî.
*B.* Nângmâ kû bûfai maund ringâh pêrrang ennî.
*S.* Nângmâ shishai maund ringâh nipêrang enni.

(4) *E.* Where shall we take the rice ?
*R.* Bûfai kôtîngmôh âtâkrâng ?
*B.* Bûfai tâkâm tâkrâng ?
*S.* Shishai kônmôh tâkrâng?

(5) *E.* Your case will be taken up to-morrow.
*R.* Nâgtûk nângmâ jông shîlrâng.
*B.* Nâgtûk nângmâ jông shîlrâng.
*S.* Nâgtûk nângmâ jông shîlrâng.

(6) *E.* Are there any fish in this river ?
*R.* Dûîdûngâh gănâ âhômmôh?
*B.* Dûîdûngâh gănâ âhômîn?
*S.* Dûîdûngâh gánâ âhômîn?

(7) *E.* In the rains there are many.
*R.* Fûrâh âtâm âhôm.
*B.* Fûrâh âtâm âhôm.
*S.* Sûrlai âtâm âhôm.

(8) *E.* Is there any sickness among you (in the village)?
*R.* Kûâh ânâ âhômmôh?
*B.* Kûâh ânâ âhômmôh?
*S.* Kûâh ânâ âhômmôh?

---

* A difference will be noticed in the word "where" in the three dialects.

(9) *E.* Bring some fowls and eggs.
*R.* Âr ârdûî hôngjôirô.
*B.* Âr ârdûî hôngjôirô.
*S.* Âr ârdûi hongjôirô.

(10) *E.* These hills are higher than those.
*R.* Âmâhaihi lâmtûng kûhaiku lâmtûng âshêôl.
*B.* Âmâhi lâmtûng kûkû lâmtûng âshôtôl.
*S.* Âmâhi lâmtûng kûkû lâmtûng âshôtôl.

(11) *E.* The deer came from the jungle.
*R.* Râmâtâ sâjûkhai âhôngtâ.
*B.* Râmâtâ sâjûkhai âhôngtâ.
*S.* Râmâta sâjûkhai âhôngtâ.

(12) *E.* I shall go: you will go: they will go.
*R.* Gêfêrâng; nângfêrâng; âmâhai fêrâng.
*B.* Gêfêrâng; nângfêrâng; âmâhai fêrâng.
*S.* Gêsêrâng; nâng sêrâng; âmâhai sêrâng.

(13) *E.* I will not come.
*R.* Gê âhông mâk (*or* nîmâk).
*B.* Gê âhông mâk.
*S.* Gê âhôngmâk.

(14) *E.* Will he not come?
*R.* Âmâ âhôngmâk môh ?
*B.* Amâ âhôngmâk môh ?
*S.* Âmâ âhôngmâk môh ?

## REMARKS.

It will have been seen from the vocabulary of the three dialects, Rángkhôl, Bêtê, and Sakajaib, that there is but little difference. The Rángkhôl "s" sometimes in Bêtê appears as "t," thus "shâmâk," "tâmâk," and "er" is replaced occasionally by "ră," a slight difference in the three is to be noticed in "earth," "fish," "husband," and a few other words.

In the sentences the words for "these" differ, but the interrogative "môh" is used in the same way. The tense terminations of the verb will be seen to be the same, as also the case termination of nouns. The plurals of nouns and pronouns are formed in identically the same manner in all three dialects.

The verb in its negative form is also used in the same manner.

# THE VOCABULARY OF JANSEN AND TADOI DIALECTS.

| *English.* | *Jansen.* | *Tadöi.* |
|---|---|---|
| Air | faigû | faigû *or* bî. |
| All | âbonâ | âbonâ. |
| Arm | îbân, kût | îbân, kût. |
| Axe | haijâ | hai. |
| Bad | âpâpôï | âpâpôï. |
| Bamboo | rômâö | rômâö. |
| Bathe | dûî gêrshil. | dûî gêrshil. |
| Bear | vômpî | vômpî. |
| Big | âtînï | âtînï. |
| Bird | âh | âh. |
| Black | âvômi | âvômi. |
| Boat | gông | gông. |
| Body | îpûmpî | îpûmpî. |
| Boy | naopang | naopang, chapong |
| Buy | jotân | jotân. |
| Cock | âhkông | âhkông. |
| Come | hôngtâng | hôngtâng. |
| Cut | sâtâng | sâtâng. |
| Day | shûnâh | shûnâh. |
| Dead | âtîtâ | âtîtâ. |
| Dog | ûî | ûî. |
| Earth | lênêng | lênêng. |
| Egg | âhdûî | âhdûî. |
| Eye | mît | mît. |
| Father | gapâ | gapâ. |
| Fire | mê | mê. |
| Fish | gănâ | gănâ. |
| Get | mân | mân. |
| Goat | gêt | gêl. |
| God | pâtin, mûnjai | pâtin. |
| Good | âpaiîngï | âpaiîngï. |
| Gun | mêpûm | mêpûm. |
| Hill | lâmtûng | lâmtûng. |
| Husband | rûâpâ | rûâpâ. |
| Iron | tî | tî. |
| Jhúm | lô | lô. |
| Kill | dêngïn | dêngïn. |
| Land | lêning | lening. |
| Large | âlîn | âlîn. |
| Man | mîhim | mîhim. |

| *English.* | *Jansen.* | *Tadoi.* |
|---|---|---|
| Moon | mîtâlâm | mîtâlâm. |
| Mother | ganû | ganû. |
| Night | jân | jân. |
| Now | toutâah | toutâah. |
| Old | âlûï | âlûï. |
| Paddy | jânghôm | janghôm. |
| Pig | vôk | vôk. |
| Rain | vû | vû. |
| Red | âsên | âsen. |
| Rice | jângshâng | jângshâng. |
| River | wâdûng | wâdûng. |
| Road | lâmpî | lâmpî. |
| Run | taitung | taitung. |
| Salt | jî | jî. |
| Shoot | kâprô | kâprô. |
| Speak | sôîtung | sôîtung. |
| Sum | tuîôh | tûîôh. |
| Tiger | hômpuï | hômpuï. |
| Tobacco | dûm | dûm. |
| To-day | tunî | tunî. |
| To-morrow | jinglê | tainî. |
| Village | kû | ku. |
| Water | duî | duî. |
| Work | boldingôme | boldingôme. |
| One | kât | kât. |
| Two | nî | nî. |
| Three | tûm | tûm. |
| Four | lî | lî. |
| Five | n̄â | n̄â. |
| Six | vûp | vûp. |
| Seven | sagî | sagî. |
| Eight | gît | gît. |
| Nine | gu | gu. |
| Ten | shôm | shôm. |
| One hundred | îâkât | îâkât. |
| One thousand | shângkât | shângkât. |

## ILLUSTRATIVE SENTENCES.

The two dialects, Jansen and Tadöi, are so alike that only one set of sentences need be given:—

(1) *English.* Where is your village?
*Jansen.* **Nâng kû kôîkômbâm?**

(2) *E.* Is the land good ?
*J.* Lêshit âpâï?
(3) *E.* Your village must supply five maunds of rice.
*J.* Nângmâ kûâh maund n͞â pêdingnâhi.
(4) *E.* Where shall we take the rice ?
*J.* Jângchâng kêïâh najôïdinghâm?
(5) *E.* Your case will be taken up to-morrow.
*J.* Nâng môkôdômâ jinglê hêdinghê.
(6) *E.* Are there any fish in this river?
*J.* Hê vôdûngâh găhâ âtâm ïngê?
(7) *E.* In the rains there are many.
*J.* Jûlê âtâm ïngė.
(8) *E.* Is there any sickness among you?
*J.* Nânghôgê nâdâm hêhə?
(9) *E.* Bring some fowls and eggs.
*J.* Áhlê âhdûi hôngjôïin.
(10) *E.* These hills are higher than those.
*J.* Himôlhi hīmôl âsângï.
(11) *E.* The deer came from the jungles.
*J.* Âgâmlââh sâjûk âhôngï.
(12) *E.* I shall go: you will go: they will go.
*J.* Gê jêngê: nâng jêding: âmâhô jêding.
(13) *E.* I will not come,
*J.* Gê âhông pông kêtê.
(14) *E.* Will he not come?
*J.* Âmâ hông lôding-hâm?

## Remarks.

The Jansen and Tadöi dialects are practically identical, and do not call for remark. It is necessary, however, to point out the difference between Jansen, Tadöi, and the Rângkhôl.

Taking the vocabulary first, we see that a large number of words are very dissimilar, though a still larger number are the same, or nearly the same, in both dialects. Very common words in every-day use, such as "all," "good," "tiger," are very different, though it was to be expected that in dialects bearing a close relation the one to the other the change would be found in the rarer words and not in those commonly used.

*Sentences.*—By the first sentence "where is your village?" Rangkhol "nâng (mâ) kû kôtïngmôh," Jansen "nâng kû kôi kômhâm" we see that in both dialects the sign of the possessive case is omitted or may be omitted. The termination "hâm" in Jansen is exactly the same as the Rangkhol interrogative "môh," and is used in the same way; but whereas in the latter it is rarely, if ever, omitted in a sentence, in the former it is very often optional.

The tense termination of the verb in Jansen differ, and agree with their persons in the singular number (*see* sentence 12).

## LUSHAI VOCABULARY.

| | |
|---|---|
| Air | klî. |
| All | âzain. |
| Arm | ban. |
| Axe | repôĭ. |
| Bad | attâlô. |
| Bamboo | mâo. |
| Bathe | buâl. |
| Bear | sâvôm. |
| Big | allîn. |
| Bird | sâvâ. |
| Black | âdûm. |
| Boat | lông. |
| Body | pûm. |
| Boy | naopong. |
| Buy | lêrô. |
| Cock | ârpâ. |
| Come | sôhôrô. |
| Cut | sâtrô. |
| Day | nî. |
| Dead | âthî. |
| Dog | ûî. |
| Earth | lê. |
| Egg | ârtûi. |
| Eye | mît. |
| Father | âpâ. |
| Fire | mê. |
| Fish | sagănâ. |
| Get | mô. |
| Goat | kêl. |
| God | pâthîn. |
| Good | âttâ. |
| Gun | sêlai. |
| Hill | klâng. |
| Husband | pâsul. |
| Iron | thîr. |
| Jhúm | so. |
| Kill | tâtrô. |
| Land | lê. |
| Large | âllîn. |
| Man | mî. |
| Moon | klâ. |
| Mother | nû. |
| Night | jân. |
| Now | zûnâ. |
| Old | âllûkî. |
| Paddy | bôhûm. |
| Pig | vôk. |
| Rain | rûâ. |
| Red | âhsên. |
| Rice | bûfai. |
| River | sôîdông. |
| Road | kâl kông. |
| Rum | klânrô. |
| Salt | chî. |
| Short | kâprô. |
| Speak | sôîrô. |
| Sum | nî. |
| Tiger | sâkêr. |
| Tobacco | vailô. |
| To-day | voĭnâ. |
| To-morrow | nûktûka. |
| Village | khûâ. |
| Water | tûi. |
| Work | nârtôkrô. |

| | | | |
|---|---|---|---|
| One | pêkât. | Seven | pâsârî. |
| Two | pânî. | Eight | pârît. |
| Three | pâtûm. | Nine | pâknâ. |
| Four | pâlî. | Ten | sôm. |
| Five | pongâ. | One hundred | jâkât. |
| Six | pârûk. | One thousand | shângkât. |

(1) Where is your village?
Nungmâ khôkhîângâ?

(2) Is the land about you good?
Lê âttâ-mô?

(3) Your village must supply five maunds of rice.
Nangmâ khûâ-mîhô bûfai pôrgănâ ânpêâng.

(4) Where shall we take the rice?
Kôilâmâ gănê bûfai kâpôrdôn?

(5) Your case will be taken up to-morrow.
In înhêk nûgtûkâ rîâng.

(6) Are there any fish in this river?
Hêmi lôîdôngâ sângâ ômêm?

(7) In the rains there are many.
Phôrhônâ âttûm ômâng.

(8) Is there any sickness among you?
Nung, mânî jîngâ ênârmô?

(9) Bring some fowls and eggs.
Ar ârtûî pôk rônpôïrô.

(1) These hills are higher than those.
Sorklâng lê hemîk lâng âsângî.

(11) The deer come from the jungle.
Râmâ tûngîn sâkî âlôhôngî.

(12) I shall go, you will go, they will go.
Kâkalâng; ekâlâng; ânkâlâng.

(13) I will not come.
Kâ kâlônâng.

(14) Will he not come?
Am-lô hôrlômô?

## Remarks.

Of the 64 words in the Lushai vocabulary 30 are identical, as regards force and meaning assigned, with those found in the Râングkhôl list. Of the remaining 34, 11 words vary but very slightly in the two dialects. There are only 23 words totally different. The Râングkhôl " s " in Lushai often appears as " t, " *viz.*, " âttâ " " good. " As compared with the Jansen vocabulary, 17 words are practically the same, and 14 differ but slightly. We thus see that more than half the words are totally distinct, and that as compared with Râugkhôl, the dialect ( Jansen ) does not bear nearly so close a resemblance. It will be noticed, however, that a few words alike in Rângkhôl and Lushai differ in Jansen, and *vice versa*. As a matter of fact, the difference is greater between the two dialects ( Jansen and Rângkhôl ) commonly called " Kuki " than between R ângkhôl and Lushai.

## Sentences.

In comparing the Rângkhôl and Lushai sentences we find a great deal in common. The interrogative "mô," "môh," * is identical, and is used much in the same manner. The three dialects, Lushai, Rângkhôl, and Jansen, are so obviously from one common parent stock, that it is not necessary to point out in detail the identical way in which they agree and in which they differ. It will have been seen that on the whole there is a far greater connection between Rângkhôl and Lushai than between Lushai and Jansen.

* I have to thank Mr. W. W. Daly, the Commandant of the Surma Valley Battalion, Frontier Police, for the Lushai vocabulary and list of sentences which he has obligingly placed at my disposal.